EAST*international*
selectors Dirk Snauwaert & Jeremy Deller
8 July to 19 August 2006

norwich gallery
norwich school of art and design

Acknowledgements

ISBN 1-872482-80-5
© 2006 Norwich Gallery Artists and Curator
Editor Lynda Morris
Design Paul Kuzemczak
Print Saxon Print Group
Edition 1000

Curator Lynda Morris
Assistant Curator Dan Tombs
Administrator Eleanor Cherry
Technicians Paul Kuzemczak and Thomas Salt

Education Ruth Ewan Dan Tombs Mandy Roberts Patricia Hall
Installation Becci Hill Charlie Crampton Dave Ramage Freddie Checketts Jay Barsby John Eadon Jonathan Allen Jonny Winter
Kaavous Clayton Lucy Conochie Malin Bjorklund Neil Baker Neil Smallbone Phil Gardner Robin Tarbet Saim Demircan Sam Halstead
Tim Fox Tristan Stevens Zeph Daniel
Invigilation Andrew McFadyen Beatrice Cowern Georgina Riley James Metsoja Jonny Winter Simon Davenport Wylie Schwartz
Selection Andrew McFadyen Emma Shipton-Smith Jonny Winter Katherine Mager Keri Lambden Lavendhri Arumugam
Sabina Checketts Simon Davenport
Interns Postgraduate Studies in Curatorial Practice and Theory Art History Institute Jagiellonian University Krakow Agnieszka Grzegorczyk
Kasia Szydlowska Curating Contemporary Art Royal College of Art Michael Polsinelli Emily Smith

Thanks Niki Braithwaite and Jane Bhoyroo Arts Council of England East the Principal and Staff of Norwich School of Art and Design
Sarah Cannell Target Follow Sheffield Hallam University The Forum Norwich Andrzej Szczerski and Adam Burdek

EASTdiscourses
October 05 Ethics into Aesthetics convenor Gustav Metzger speakers Cornelia Parker Doug Fishbone Gustav Metzger Immo Klink
John Wood Lee Holden Max Vollmer Mark Wilsher Melissa Bliss Nicola Foster Peter Kennard & Cat Picton-Philips Peter Suchin
February 06 Adam Latham David Brazier Duncan Swann Haris Epaminonda Hewitt & Jordan Jarrett Mitchell John Duncan John Goodwin
John Lloyd & Kate Williams Keith Farquhar Kevin Hutcheson Mark Boulos Masayuki Suzuki Matt Stokes Tom Ranahan Rebecca Birch
Roman Vasseur Rory Macbeth Rosie Snell Ruth Ewan Theresa Nanigian Yara El-Sherbini

EASTsteering committee
Chair Simon Willmoth Lynda Morris Roger Ackling Niki Braithwaite ACE:E Manuel Chetcuti Barbara Howey Sarah Horton
Nichola Johnson SCVA Mark Wilsher Nav Haq Andrew Moore NCMAG Mary Muir Norfolk County Council
Nikki Rotsos Norwich City Council Rebecca Weaver Ipswich Borough Council Paul Kuzemczak co-opted Eleanor Cherry Dan Tombs

  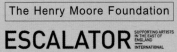   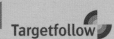

EASTinternational
selectors Dirk Snauwaert & Jeremy Deller
8 July to 19 August 2006

Adam Latham
Chris Evans
David Brazier
Duncan Swann
Freee
Haris Epaminonda
Jarrett Mitchell
John Duncan
John Goodwin
John Lloyd & Kate Williams
Keith Farquhar
Kevin Hutcheson
Mark Boulos
Masayuki Suzuki
Matt Stokes
Nate Harrison
Rebecca Birch
Roman Vasseur
Rory Macbeth
Rosie Snell
Ruth Ewan
Theresa Nanigian
Tom Ranahan
Vaast Colson
Yara El-Sherbini

norwich gallery
norwich school of art and design

Lord Mayor of Norwich, Councillor Felicity Hartley said, "Norwich is the Cultural Capital of the East of England. EAST International is the region's and indeed one of Britain's leading annual exhibitions of contemporary art.

I am honoured to be featured, in my role as Lord Mayor, as part of the exhibition on a cloth bag - or as my friends have so eloquently put it, I can now take retail therapy to the limit!"

EAST*international* 2006
Introduction

The structure of an **EAST** exhibition allows artists to tell us what is going on. The selectors reflect what they learn from looking at around 7,000 slides by 1,100 artists from more than 30 countries.

We have had to overcome criticism of open shows and find the way to attract good artists to **EAST**. This has been done by the choice of selectors who are respected by artists. Accepting our invitation means, by definition, they have stayed on the side of the artist.

Over the last 16 years **EAST** has reinvigorated the idea of open submission exhibitions. The trust of artists in the democratic structure of an open exhibition has enabled **EAST** to make a gentle annual reminder of the artists "out there".

Artists today have been educated in Post-Modern Theory, which has replaced historical and documentary memory. In this exhibition the idea of the artist as a moral force has reappeared – with a lightness of touch. Musicians, filmmakers, writers and artists are reclaiming progressive traditions and forms of expression.

Changes in an era appear first in the work of individual artists. They tell us about the times we are living through. Goethe told us that: "All eras in a state of decline and dissolution are subjective; on the other hand all progressive eras have an objective tendency." **EAST** is a word with many meanings as the reference in the artists' work makes clear: East/West, Eastern Europe, the Eastern Mediterranean, the Near East, the Middle East, the East India Company, the Far East, the Hippy East as well as East Anglia.

ARTISTS

We hold an **EAST***discourse* each year where most of the artists selected for the exhibition make a preliminary visit to Norwich and show slides of their work to each other and our immediate audience. This introduction to their work is largely based on that discourse held this year on 10 February 2006 and the notes on it Eleanor Cherry and I made. Bringing the artists together with our immediate audience here in Norwich, means the artists in the exhibition, and the artists who work on installing **EAST**, have the same insider knowledge as the selectors and the curator.

One of the major off site projects for **EAST** is **Rory Macbeth's** transformation of a building with the text of Thomas More's *Utopia*. In Greek *Utopia* means *No Place*, not paradise. This Utopia project involves the artist writing the entire text of Sir Thomas More's *Utopia* on the outside of a free-standing building, ready for demolition. Sarah Cannell of Target Follow helped us to find a de-commissioned electrical sub station in the old telephone exchange in Duke Street, which runs parallel to St Georges Street. It is difficult to describe Macbeth's work; some of it is collaborative, such as the fake student he enrolled into the Foundation course at Central St. Martin's with Laura Lord; or as 'The Brians Sewell' with Darren Phizacklea, where amongst other work inspired by the infamous critic, they produced "Waxwork of a Brian Sewell Lookalike". As a member of Twentieth Century he has shown at the ICA's 'Berlin/London01', where the group installed a karaoke version of "Take My Breath Away" by Berlin, translated by computer into german and back into english, making it nonsense. They also applied the same double-translation software to make nonsense of all the computer networks in the ICA for the duration of the show. He installed 40 workmans' radios in a gallery and an applause machine at the door of another gallery. He made bronze trophy-sized sculptures of heroes and heroines of performance art including Beuys and Kline. He re-sprays abandoned cars and motorbikes to make them look nice again. He recorded 5 covers of utopian songs by people whose lives have been far from ideal, done in a style that preceded the original: the Beach Boys as early Ska, John Lennon as early Motown. He also re-arranged the words of the Bible in alphabetical order.

Ruth Ewan made *A Colouring Book of People Trying to Stop the War* in 2001 while she was a student at Edinburgh College of Art. It was based on the Black Panthers Colouring Book she had come across. The Black Panthers created a free breakfast program, serving young black and low-income children across America and there was concern that the program spread anti-white propaganda. The book was in fact a pre-emptive strike created by the FBI's Counter Intelligence Program. The program hoped to neutralise organisations that posed a perceived threat to American society, for example the Black Panthers, Communists and Labour Union Leaders, Anti-Vietnam peaceniks and Native American Groups. It was the FBI's idea of a 24 page colouring book of anti white propaganda made to look as though it was by the Black Panthers. Ruth's colouring book, which featured images from anti-war demonstrations, was distributed to local children. For her *Psittaciformes Trying to*

Change the World project shown at the Embassy in Edinburgh and Studio Voltaire in London she attempted to teach parrots phrases recorded at the protests surrounding the July 2005 G8 Summit. Two of the parrots now shout the word 'revolution'. Certain parrots, particularly African Greys, have shown evidence of processing and understanding information. For **EAST** she began by researching the social history of Norwich: 'I came across the story of Robert Kett, who led the Norfolk Rising in 1549 over the fencing off of common land by the local gentry. For a short period, before he was executed at Norwich Castle, Kett declared and held a people's parliament under what is now know as 'The Oak of Reformation' on Mousehold Heath.' With support from the Arts Council she has commissioned a song entitled *The Rebels' Complaint* based on the legend of Kett, co-written and performed by Fay Fife, the lead singer of the 1970s Scottish punk band, The Rezillos. Ruth hopes the song will enter popular culture in order to disseminate the legacy of Robert Kett.

The identification of form with content means Los Angeles artist **Nate Harrison's** *Can I Get An Amen?*, is itself a record of his fascination with a drum break called the 'Amen Break' the 1960s track *Amen Brother* by The Winstons. Their break in the drum roll has become a stock phrase in mixes for recent recordings and its use in music, from Rap and Hip-Hop to commercial adverts, has been without acknowledgement of copyright. At **EAST** *Can I Get an Amen?* will be available for visitors to play on a Technics Turntable. Copies of *Can I Get An Amen?* will be on sale at the exhibition, copyrighted and signed by the artist.

Matt Stokes' practice is marked by anthropological enquiry and an interest in events or informal movements that bind people together. His projects have included *Long After Tonight* (2005), a film commissioned by Dundee Contemporary Arts, which documents a Northern Soul session staged in the ornate nave of St Salvador's Church, parts of which were used during the 1970's for the city's first 'Northern' nights. For *Sacred Selections* (ongoing), he brings together contrasting communities via a series of live pipe organ recitals. The performances feature music chosen by people from different underground music cultures strongly associated with the north of Britain; Northern Soul, Happy Hardcore and Black Metal. Transcriptions of the original tracks were carried out with the support of the Royal College of Organists. For **EAST** Stokes has organised an extension of the three concerts, incorporating additional music and research into the history of pipe organs of the city. The performances will be held at; St Peter Mancroft Church (Northern Soul), United Reformed Church (Happy Hardcore) and St Andrews Hall (Black Metal), and organists include David Dunnett from Norwich Cathedral. A small practice organ, built by Peter Collins, will also be installed at **EAST**, where local organists can try out the three sets of scores. Stokes has previously exhibited with Grizedale Arts (Cumbria), Workplace (Gateshead), and he was awarded the Beck's Futures 2006 prize, at the ICA in London.

The Australian artist **David Brazier** has organised Norwich's Strongest Man and Woman Competition for **EAST**. The value of being physically "strong" is almost irrelevant in today's society, bringing a humorous redundancy to the competition. By placing an arm wrestling competition within the context of an open submission art exhibition he aims to juxtapose the heroics of professional sport with the aesthetics of minimalism. Jeremy Deller suggested holding the competition in the city centre before the opening to attract a non-arts based local community to **EAST**. This will happen on Hay Hill on Saturday 17 June from 12 to 4pm. With new funding from the Arts Council, T-shirts are being printed, there will be badges for competitors and a new arm wrestling table has been commissioned. £100 prizes will be presented as oversized cheques to the winner of each category. David Brazier designed a poster to advertise the event to gyms around the city and has made contact with the police and fire brigade. The exhibition space will contain photographs, video highlights and signage from the competition as well as the custom made arm wrestling table so people can have a go themselves.

Masayuki Suzuki is from Japan and he currently lives and works in London. He has studied various martial arts for over 20 years, including two years in a US Air Force Base teaching martial arts. He is interested in computer games' artificial scenes, distorting the sense of violence and creating an artificial sense of distance between the player and the consequences of the act committed. He thinks the reason for the increase in child violence, for example 'happy slapping' is the distortion created by computer games of an artificial distance between the player and the act committed. His works asks the questions of: what is real, what is pain, what is scary? He uses his own body as a tool to explore and highlight these issues. For **EAST** he will perform *Majestic Boy* martial arts on people attending the opening. He is particularly interested in finding girls who he can get to 'throw' him. Documentation of the performance at the opening of **EAST** will be shown in the exhibition. He studied art in Japan, where he learnt traditional wood carving. **EAST** has been a point of entry for several Japanese artists, including Tomoko Takahashi, Tazro Niscino and Hiraki Sawa.

Freee is the art collective of Hewitt, Jordan and Beech, based in Sheffield and London. Freee work with art, language and politics: *The Economic Function of Public Art is to Increase the Value of Private Property* and *Artists cannot bring integrity to your project unless they provide a full and candid critique of everything you do*. They are interested in projects, teaching, curating, collaborations, intervention, action, performance, art institutions, public realm, social change, conflict, agency and transformation. They claim negation is positive. They hope to contest culture and assert a way to encourage: *Public Art for Public Good*. For **EAST** they will recreate their billboard: *"The Economic Function of Public Art is to Increase the Value of Private Property"*.

The Flemish artist **Vaast Colston** works with performances based on memories of his childhood. He has returned to the scene of holiday photographs with his parents and brother and made a trip of rediscovery of the years they spent as a family in Australia. In **EAST** his installation will be an archive of his performances as an introduction to his work for UK audiences. The archive will be housed in a construction that owes something to his years as a skateboarder used to makeshift constructions. He too will produce a multiple, a CD disc of *Ten Fibs I Told as a Child* and an invitation to respond to them. The multiple has to be found so you have to search the Bars and Clubs of Norwich. Remember: *Though A Lie be swift, the truth overtakes it.*

John Duncan has been based in Belfast for the last 14 years. **EAST** will show a retrospective selection of the work that examines the post-ceasefire transformation of Belfast. In the earliest work 'Boom Town' we see cleared urban spaces in which developers' hoardings give a view of the apartments, offices and civic buildings yet to be constructed, along with the lifestyles we can expect to be enjoyed in them. With the construction of these buildings new interfaces have been created between them and the existing communities in the city. An image from 'Trees from Germany', a series exploring these tensions, shows the lawn in front of the New Days Hotel being rolled out towards a Loyalist Paramilitary Mural. The most recent series 'We were here' looks at the demilitarisation that is taking place as part of the peace process. At Girdwood Army Barracks in North Belfast successive army regiments marked their tour of duty by painting operational banners on the internal walls of the base. During the handover to civilian contractors dismantling the base these have been painted out. The work documents these walls as part of an ongoing project registering the steady appearance of a new Belfast.

Rosie Snell's fascination with the military began while she was a student in Norwich a decade ago. Passing military establishments in East Anglia she became fascinated by the sight of military machines in the landscape. Beautifully designed objects that are killing machines. In her paintings the woodland foliage forms a zone between the motif, acting both as cover and as a barrier denying us access. Nature breaks down and emulates the deception and concealment of camouflage. Camouflage confuses reality with fiction as a form of censorship. Recent military scholarship about R.M.A. the *Revolution in Military Affairs* is about warfare in the Information Age. Increasingly, concepts and capabilities associated with the Information Age, such as *Dominant Battle Space Knowledge*, *Strategic Information Warfare*, and *Unmanned Aerial Vehicles*, seem to offer a potential new type of warfare, a post-heroic warfare without bloodshed. It is now thought possible to remove the human factor altogether by using *Artificial Intelligence*. Information dominance could render force redundant, so warfare may increasingly be characterized by hide and seek. Or not. Baudrillard compares modern warfare to Hollywood film scripts. Electronic warfare involves new forms of deception, by means of electronic interference and falsified signals. It becomes possible to employ the mass media to pass disinformation, lies and propaganda. TV claims to provide immediate access to real events, whereas in fact it produces information that stands in for the real.

The six glass sculptures of nuclear power stations are the first time **John Lloyd + Kate Williams** have collaborated. They have received an Arts Council Commission and Kate Williams has been working with Northlands Creative Glass in Caithness Scotland. Together they have been making a large Vaseline glass sculpture of Dounreay Nuclear Power Station, lit by ultra violet light. We plan to show this piece in the *The Forum* in Norwich. Their sculptures include Sizewell Nuclear Power Station A & B between Ipswich and Southwold. Springfield Nuclear Power Station from the Simpson's and Doel Nuclear Power Station in Belgium.

East Anglia's changing coastline is the subject of **Rebecca Birch's** conversations with people whose homes are threatened by coastal erosion. In the past decade government coastal management policy has begun to look at *managed retreat* from some coastal areas to allow space for sea levels to rise. She looks at the impact of this policy on a community in North Norfolk that has lost sea defences. In the recordings people talk about living with an eroding coastline, continuing to run businesses and attempt to plan for the future as their back gardens begin to fall. As their homes move closer to the edge they may have a better view of the sea but their uncertainty is revealed in small changes to regular patterns. They now plant runner beans as they only take 6 months to grow rather than asparagus that takes 3 years.

Keith Farquhar lives and works in Edinburgh. Recently he has made major sculptural installations in New York and Edinburgh. *Atomised* takes its name from the Michel Houellebecq novel in which the malaise within contemporary masculine culture is put right through human cloning and the end of individuality consists of a room of faceless figures made from pristine 'Off the peg' white hoodies and dark indigo Levis Jeans, vacuously gazing at a huge totem of 200 of the same folded white hoodies. It is as if the clothes which have been made into figures are telepathically willing life into the yet to be animated, material of their own making. An installation called *Nice Pair of Trainers, Shoes, Jeans and a Top* made for Inverleith House in Edinburgh (also illustrated) continues with the dress-codes of contemporary male youth and has the grand, Georgian building squatted with these same forlorn hooded figures - this time gazing at a massive denim frieze which forms a Rothko-like landscape from a hugely oversized jean turn-up which encompasses all three rooms of the downstairs gallery. Most recently for the exhibition *Dada's Boys* at the Fruitmarket Gallery, Edinburgh, Farquhar was the only artist amongst an all-star cast to be commissioned to make a new work. He responded with another large scale installation entitled *The Rules of Attraction:(White Wine/White cotton)* in which hugely oversized glasses, containing ultra-lifelike, theatrical white wine, acted as figures in a contemporary mating ritual. Crudely dunked Calvin Klein female underwear appeared to represent a sexual conquest had taken place within an arena entirely encompassed by IKEA mirrors. For **EAST** Farquhar is currently working with brand new jeans which enter the high street store deliberately distressed - a comment on our post industrial age where the lack of manual work and fashion's ever increasing turnover speed means that clothes never have the chance to actually wear out. **The Idle:(Denim in Distress)** will be shown in the Norwich Gallery with its shop window facing onto the street between Norwich's up-town and down-town.

Chris Evans creates scenarios that take the form of events, sculptures and airbrush paintings: These works, to date, include the following: where he employs old sculptors who built monuments in Estonia during the era of soviet-occupation to build a new sculpture park from the radically loyal corporate imagination of directors of companies like Starbucks and Chrysler; where there might be something we could name 'The Freedom of Negative Expression'; where he sets up an Existentialist retreat called 'Militant Bourgeois' for over-subsidised Dutch art students so they can experience dread in order to make better work; where he works on behalf of all artists in obtaining funding from institutions for projects related to trees, and where the 'Friends of the Divided Mind' can re-unite in a park in a small town in Scotland. Recently, Evans has been arranging for national police forces to go on a recruiting run of European art colleges. **EAST** will be assisting Evans in setting up future 'Coptalks' in the next academic year. In addition, Evans will be presenting the latest development of his work 'A Sculpture for the Ahmed Family' - part of a series that Evans is making where he seeks to represent the ideas of the 'elite' in sculptural forms.

A dark side of history informs the work of **Roman Vasseur.** He transported a meter cube crate of earth from Transylvania, to the Austrian Culture Forum in Knightsbridge. One inspiration for the work was the film *The Revenge of Count Yorga* that had a shot of a crate travelling up an L.A. highway. A Western myth, describing an East/West paradigm. Another film *Under Fire* inspired a leaflet drop from a small airplane near Joshua Tree in Texas, shown daily on a local TV channel. He worked in Public Arts Curation and Administration and attempted to stop community arts projects happening. He lives on the St George's Estate in London, a classic Greater London County Council designed set of buildings. When he came back from USA he found a 125-foot wall mural had been painted on a wall that could be viewed from their homes by the majority of tenants. He considered it state sponsored vandalism that typically devalues the places where people live. He tried to fund the removal of the mural, applying for an Arts Council grant to do this. He thinks that this kind of public art has a latent violence at work within it. He subsequently proposed the ritual sacrifice of the artist and curator responsible for this mural and other public artworks. He suggested that they would take part in the sacrifice willingly, as they would accept that their deaths would provide a site for a more effective coming together of the community. At **EAST**, in the School where he first studied, he will paint a mural of his own.

In her video *46 missed manicures*, American artist **Theresa Nanigian** considers the devastating effects of 9:11 from quite a different perspective to that reflected in popular media. Having moved from New York City to Dublin only shortly before the terrorist attacks occurred, she portrays a more intimate and personal loss by documenting the secondary effects of this horrific incident. In keeping with her practice of borrowing from the tools and aesthetics of various analytical systems, Nanigian employs the language of commerce and its frequent use of analytical facts and figures to create an inventory that goes beyond cold, hard statistics and charts the human-scale consequences of such a catastrophic event.

Mark Boulos is from Boston USA but now lives and works in London. He is a filmmaker primarily interested in the religion and the conflict between the West and the Middle East. He says he attempts to invert documentary through the lens of religion. Most documentary films report objective facts, but his show a truth that is radically subjective: belief so devout that it becomes real. His films portray people in the throes of religious ecstasy or political militancy to the point that they want to sacrifice themselves to become either martyrs or saints. For example, "Jerusalem" portrays Abu Hamza preaching terrorism on the street outside Finsbury Park Mosque, while "The Gates of Damascus" follows a Syrian housewife who receives stigmata and revelations over Easter weekend. For **EAST** he is creating a new film, commissioned by the Arts Council and the British Documentary Film Foundation. He has filmed in the last Christian village in Syria where Aramaic, Christ's vernacular, is still spoken, and also in a Pentecostal Church in London, where the faithful 'speak-in-tongues' when they pray.

Yara El-Sherbini uses humour to make socially engaged work, which manifests itself in multiple ways, including visual and verbal puns. Two culturally and socially specific works, which explore being a Muslim woman in the context of culture and British-ness, are firstly the jokes she makes and installs as text pieces, and secondly her stand-up comedy routine, documentation of which will be shown at **EAST** *Avoiding Dark Ali's*. Her work, which focuses on language, includes interactive artworks where text

responds to voice to alter words, such as turning *Bullsh*it into *Bush*. and *Manifesto*, a playful public declaration of her principles and objectives. *Manifesto* will be shown at **EAST**. Her joke book *Sheikh 'n' Vac* was commissioned by Bookworks in 2005.

In our fractured culture *collage* is a strong force for modern image making. The Glasgow artist **Kevin Hutcheson** makes collages using magazine cuttings and vintage imagery of counter cultural icons such as David Bowie, Peter Fonda, Joe Orton and Kenneth Halliwell. Other works present oblique texts sometimes touched with paint, very slight but particularly memorable. One collage imagines a cat from the perspective of a blind person. He has shown work with Jack Hanley in San Francisco and Hotel in London. The work is fragile and one suspects the artist is connecting with the hidden depths of a Calvinist conscience. We commissioned *Looted* as a signed poster because it was just so stunning. Glasgow keeps producing these artists.

The Cypriot artist **Haris Epaminonda**, born in Nicosia, the only remaining militarily divided European city, moved to London in 1997 and graduated from the Royal College of Art in 2003. Her collages, in which she reconstructs images taken from pictorial magazines of the 1950's, appear to point towards a post-human world in which the very syntax of life has become hopelessly dissembled. They seem to be touching the realm of dreams and even bizarre children's stories. The work is curious, it embraces the 'surreal' but remains at the same time at a safe distance from it, and so appears as if contained within itself, as if already disclosing, refusing to be named either in this or that way. In her video 'Nemesis 52', once again we are driven into a mysteriously double-world. A fragmentation between reality and fiction, where ambiguous objects take shape and transmute into hybrid forms that seem to have lost a sense of frontier: improbable configurations beyond definition, perfectly imaginary, and, being in two places at once almost always, residing within a state of exile.

Like any normal father, **John Goodwin** took lots of photographs of his children as they were growing up. The photographs are of the street where they lived in the Wally Range area of Manchester. The intimacy of his images is because they are photographs of his children and their close friends. The setting is his back garden and the terraced street with all the busy comings and goings. He thinks of his work as photographs of 'moments between moments'. He talks about the trial separations between the image and imagination, the fatigue of image saturation and his continuing interest in people's snapshot. The documentary tradition of photojournalism has become public property and re-invigorated by the camera-phone in almost everyone's pocket. Vilem Flusser's idea that people see photographs as windows on the world rather than images. He acknowledges television as a source of his work. He recently moved from Manchester to work at Plymouth University and that has given him a perspective on this work.

Tom Ranahan's parents moved from Ireland to Birmingham in the 60s. He struggled with his British and Irish identity growing up in the 1970s at the time of the Birmingham pub bombings. Birmingham is in a constant state of redevelopment. Artists' studios, and their pubs are often in the undeveloped areas as well as the old factories, workshops and shop that have become his subject matter. The Arts Council commissioned him to make new work for **EAST**, developing the group of photographs he made last year in Great Yarmouth. The subject that comes though is not so much the place, as Ranahan's sense of the outsider.

The themes of history and collage appear in the paintings of **Adam Latham** who graduated from painting course at Royal College of Art in 2005. He worked on an exchange in Canada where he was snowed in and spent a lot of time watching cartoons teaching himself how to draw cartoons. He made a video of a burning snowman. Music is an influence and he has made a recording for **EAST**.
His paintings are of grotesque, excessive landscapes, gloss on board paintings of huts and shacks, incorporating fairy lights. His drawings of interiors are inspired by grubby student accommodation. His portrait drawings depict people with vegetable facial features or echoes, down the decades, of a hippy East for **EAST**.

Duncan Swann graduated from the Royal College of Art in 2004. Originally from Sheffield he has lived and painted in London for the last 8 years. The paintings deal with power and domination in Western Colonialism and British Foreign Policy. They depict actual and imagined scenes from a colonial past, acting as an entry point for contemporary concerns. His imagery is of the human aspects of greed, naivety and folly. He uses images of colonial subjects from 19th and 20th century newspapers, animals and birds he has found on the Internet and in National Geographic magazines. He also uses the photographic archives at the British Library, especially images of the British in India. Frequently the paintings are underpinned by a gentle satire; the birds in the images often confront the viewer with knowing looks, as the human protagonists stumble through exotic landscapes unaware of the threats contained therein. The past and the future merge, Colonial Africa, the swamps of Borneo, the Wild West and apocalyptical visions of our own making. The grand old tradition of oil painting and popular cartoons are morphed into a vision of the primitivism of the West.

Jarrett Mitchell lives in Louisville, Kentucky and has created "The Dawn of The Birth of The Battle of The Right To Life VS. The Law of Death" for **EAST** 06. Starting with the American white tailed deer as a point of examination, Mitchell forces the iconic deer through the various cultural filters at work in North America. From the ancient Peyote tribes of the American Southwest, who believed that the deer fed on their agrarian corn, and in turn left the psychedelic substance peyote in their foot prints, to the current American suburban quagmire, whose constant encroachment upon the deer's habitat, has generated a massive spike in deadly human/deer interactions. The installation features a taxidermied deer, recovered from an auto collision; a video of interviews about human interaction with deer, including collisions and a man who raised a deer, as well as documents of deer collision fatalities and a site specific installation intended to be a god for deer. The two paintings are based on Native American weavings that use the peyote button as their psychedelic centerpiece.

Lynda Morris
June 2006

Adam Latham
born 1981 Lancaster
studied Royal College of Art
lives and works London

Heather 2006 ink on paper 85 x 55 cm

9 Million Bicycles 2006 gloss on board 183 x 213 cm

Desserted Hut 2006 gloss on board with fairylights 183 x 183 cm

Assemblage(ii) 2006 gloss on canvas 122 x 183 cm

untitled (sketchbook image) 2006

Bossa-Nova 2005 size variable latex, balloons, speaker, amplifier and cd player

Adam Latham creates drawings in ink that have the appearance of old etchings or sepia photographs. They take influence from comic artists such as Robert Crumb and their sentiments are often confused, the image filled with a mass of jumbled information. These drawings, executed with stunning care and delicacy, address complex social issues in a clumsy and ham-fisted manner. The work is given a disturbing edge by the uncertainty of the artist's position on controversial issues like racism.

Latham also produces paintings overloaded with gloss paint in sickly sweet candy colours. These paintings use imagery that, as with the drawings, contain elements of the grotesque. In many cases the work alludes to some kind of exoticism and Latham deliberately uses themes that reflect a distinctly amateur view of art.

As well as drawings and paintings Latham has previously produced giant modelling-balloon sculptures that hang from ceiling to floor slowly revolving as though floating in mid air. At the centre of the sculptures is a speaker from which a soundtrack resonates. These soundtracks have included a mournful bossa-nova Casio keyboard piece and a sombre rehashing of Mariah Carey's *"All I Want For Christmas Is You"* Over time these knotted balloon monsters sag and fall apart. In this way the sculptures are a cheeky response to Jeff Koons and the commodification of art but they also have about them something of the existential pain of Kafka's Gregor Samsa or the story of John Merrick.

All the work is characterised by excess whether through the use of material, the use of colour or the amount of labour put into its production. The tone of the work flips between facetiousness and sincerity. Sensitivity co-exists with the absurd, which produces a tension that is heightened by the artist's tasteless choice of subject matter.

Dave Benson Phillips

Chris Evans
born 1967 Eastrington
studied Leicester and Barcelona
lives and works Berlin and London
Represented by STORE London and Galerie Juliette Jongma Amsterdam
www.chrisevans.info

Chris Evans has been arranging for national police forces to go on a recruiting run of European art colleges. The first took place at the Reitveld Academy in Amsterdam in 2005, the second at Manchester Metropolitan University in March 2006 during the British Art Show. Representatives from national police forces are invited to illustrate the opportunities within such a career and encourage students to join up. For a country to have an effective police force, its constituent employees should reflect the demographics of its society. It is perhaps inevitable that members of arts communities are under-represented in the nations policing and this presentation is an attempt to address this situation and to begin to reverse this bias. From the perspective of art educational institutions, only a small proportion of art and design students continue to pursue a career directly linked to their studies. The recruitment talk should highlight the necessity for students to consider, at an early stage, what alternative careers they might go on to pursue, whilst acknowledging the asset of non-vocational study and how it can enrich the creativity, thought production, quality and value within the sectors of service, commerce and government. **EAST** will be assisting Evans in setting up future 'Cop Talks' in the next academic year.

In addition, Evans will be presenting the latest development of his work 'A Sculpture for the Ahmed Family' - part of a series that Evans is making with people around the world who we would regard as belonging to their country's 'elite'. Evans visited Justice Refaat Ahmed, in his home in Dhaka, and questioned him about his family's influence on Bangladesh - and what in effect the elite can have in relationship to, or in tandem with, the countrys faltering democracy. Refaat Ahmed talked about "rising above all that is commonplace and forging a neutral and passive path through the polarities" and the idea of a Banyan tree was proposed by his mother who was drawn to its quality of endurance. Whilst making the first maquette Evans wrote to Refaat Ahmed, explaining that he had learnt that the Banyan tree is also known as a *Strangler Fig* because it's roots gradually spread round a host tree, eventually causing that host to decay away, leaving no trace behind, except sometimes a long hollow extending up inside the middle of the full-grown Banyan. On the plus side, the Banyan is not particular about which tree it starts life on (consequently killing very few of any particular kind) and so is no threat to the survival of other plant species. Refaat Ahmed replied acknowledging the tree's "insidious trait" and hoped that it would not detract from the benevolent picture his mother was attempting to draw in using the analogy. He also clarified the term "polarities", he had used in their conversation, as "ideological polarities in a nascent democracy". Evans made a second maquette of the sculpture in response. In this latest version, exhibited in **EAST**, the Banyan tree is circling it's host but has not reached the ground to take root.

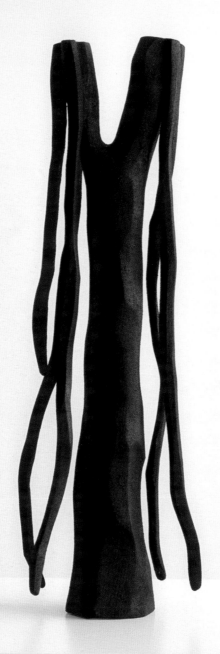

Sculpture for the Ahmed Family

Cop Talk
A recruitment talk by Waseem Ahmedi of the Greater Manchester Police Force to students of the Faculty of Fine Art Manchester Metropolitan University 16 March 2006

David Brazier
born 1974 Perth Australia
studied Curtin University Perth and Ecole Nationale Superieure des Beaux Arts Paris
studied with David Jones and Richard Deacon
lives and works London

Roman Road's Strongest Man and Woman Competition Bow Festival 2005

Duncan Swann
born 1969 Bridport
studied Royal Collage of Art
lives and works London

Of Now and Then: Notes on the Paintings of Duncan Swann

'The world is not dialectical – it is sworn to extremes, not equilibrium, sworn to radical antagonism, not reconciliation or synthesis.' Jean Baudrillard

After having spent a substantial period working within the mechanisms of a large financial company, Duncan Swann became acutely aware of the suspicion that his existence could no longer restrict itself with the sole goal of financial enterprise, life has a wider scope of possibilities. This compelled him to undertake an exploration, albeit aided by the disenchantment born from his insights and experience of the world of high finance. He cleared his desk, left the office, and embarked on a new voyage, unknown to him at the time that this chance cartography would lead to painting. As a child he would pass the time occupying himself by copying images of birds and animals, but not until he was in his early thirties as an MA student at the Royal College, would he seriously re-encounter the universe of the picture plane and develop his visual metaphors.

His early paintings reveal existentialist moments in depictions of unpeopled athletic tracks rendered in a fusion of sunset and electric floodlights, illuminating a space where the stopwatch is momentarily suspended awaiting the competitive individual to reach their 'Personal Best' (2002) in the democratic space of track and field. He soon moved into 'grid works', small square panels composed of interrelating elements depicting enigmatic, empty landscapes frozen in time, where one's point of view is a road forming vanishing points and distant horizon lines. A narrative journey into the unknown, an 'Event' (2004).

Swann's new work still uses landscape, however, the subtle, personal socio-politics of the previous paintings has been augmented with a satirical edge, which aims a critique at western expansion and its colonial histories. Gone are the grid lines and open architectural spaces, his current landscape is a dense, almost claustrophobic jungle evoking a cacophony of birds, bees, beetles and other unimaginable creatures from equatorial regions.

The plants, trees and birds are transplanted from all over the world, discovered in obscure South American prints, second hand books on conquest and exploration, and the British Library photographic collection – an atlas of imagery. In the jungle paintings we find 'protagonists', men dressed in safari suits and carrying rifles, they have brought the 'civilizing' effect of Europe into Africa and Asia.

The Honeyseekers 2005 oil on board 122.5 cm x 107cm

They are the heroic breed of explorers leading expeditions to exotic places, killing animals from Pole to Equator, a symbolic and actual demonstration of skill and prowess. These conquerors are brought back to us from the 1800s, through the time machine of appropriation. Swann re-contextualises this visual material creating a dark mood, where danger lurks in these surroundings of 'otherness' to the detriment of the protagonists. Their postures, frozen for the record, their feet firmly planted on the piled up bodies of soon to be acephalous tigers captured on the photographic parchment of semi-permanence, only to be re-captured 100 years later in a contemporary painting, their faces, pompous, hard and boring, humourless, pretentious and oblivious to their surroundings, however, on closer inspection, some of these protagonists have

Dreams of Owning the World 2006 oil on linen 180cm x 160cm

expressions of fear on their faces, as if a sudden realisation has dawned on them, a sudden petrifying lucidity, the atmosphere is an uncanny mixture of déjà vu, doubling, replication and the repetitions of loss through colonisation and the domination of people and nature.

These suspended moments are archaic, but still within the time line of modern history. This anachronism attempts to create a timeless quality to the work – 'to remove time from the historical' to be less specific about time and exist just outside living memory. In this case the use of landscape clearly becomes a concept entrenched in the past and present, it is a concept in-between time and history, space and place, an amalgam of myth, and actual event. Of course landscape does not exist in a theoretical vacuum, it takes up the dynamics or the sophistication of today's age. Today's 'landscape' is inevitably in a state of perpetual transformation, integral to processes of globalisation, objectification and the sedimentation of history.

We are in an accelerated scientific and technological approach to the natural world while, at the same time, continually breeching geographic boundaries, we are miniaturising the globe, perpetuating the un-nerving and unsettling condition of the world. This condition is the legacy of early colonial histories despots, viceroys, priests, military interventionists, and mercantilist adventurers, all equally responsible in the collaborative aim to bring us to the pan-global capitalism of today, with its 'fatal strategy' of topographic homogenisation and political double standards.

Today our mercantile adventures have a different way and their devastating strategies are somewhat out of sight, from time to time materialising in the cathode of nullifying media. Forget the galleon ships and map makers of old, now the heavily edited communication satellites aloft in the stratospheric environs of the planet, plot out this 'new' world map. Meanwhile back on the ground the combatative tentacles of the west meet the east in a plural state of co-anaesthesia like two virulent viruses mutating into one, time and space is in the market place for 'positive products' apathy and disinformation. This is the sub-text of Swann's paintings

Describing himself as a humanist, Swann addresses the negative effects of political power, already having a clear understanding of the cause and effect of economic history. He has deliberately steered away from the dry empirical or pedagogic rigors of social and political fact, purely to avoid a polemical 'preaching to the converted', believing that 'being overtly political in art may be detrimental' since political rhetoric whether semantic or semiotic is propaganda and tends to be a set of empty promises, signs or gestures, never the less, a political consciousness is at work in the paintings articulation and engagement with economic history.

Through reading maverick philosophers such as Cornelius Castoriadis and Elias Canetti, the literature of Joseph Conrad and Gabriel Garcia Marquez, Swann situates his work within a poetic framework, rather than be bombastic in his imagery he prefers to create a 'critique' that is ambiguous. Swann understands the problematic tropes of ambiguity and appropriation, but consciously uses these visual tactics, believing that it facilitates for the viewer, an open access point to the paintings subject matter, to hold focus on the speculative quality inherent in the image, to explore the ambiguity and find the tension of dichotomy – cause and effect, malevolent exploiter, benevolent explorer, entropic utopianism or, a revival of liberalism.

The New Explorers 2006 oil on linen 25 cm x 20.5cm

It is useful to have a concept that is free from an absolutely fixed position, where meaning can be elusive or ambiguous, yet the potential range is all encompassing. Landscape is a frame for discourse that encourages the development of metaphors, which enables the exploration of old and universal topics in new ways, and which may provide the framework for the construction of new theories, new hopes, and the eventual break with the circularity of destructive reoccurrences, currently the only true testament to man's absurd inability to learn from his mistakes. Until this break...time is indefinitely suspended.

© L B 2006

The Matriarch 2005 oil on linen 183 cm x 153 cm

Freee

Hewitt, Jordan and Beech work collectively as Freee

公共藝術中的新帝國主義

The neo-imperialist function of public art is to clear a path for aggressive economic expansion

E為急進的經濟擴張開路

Freee

Hewitt, Jordan and Beech work collectively as Freee

Haris Epaminonda
born 1980 Nicosia Cyprus
studied Royal College of Art
lives and works Nicosia and London
represented by Domobaal London
www.harisepaminonda.com

Untitled 1 (The Passers) 2005-06 collage 24 x 23 cm

Gesture between Worlds
Excerpt from an essay by Jonathan Miles
Domobaal editions London 2006

'It is strange that I am talking to you about the work of old men. Perhaps this is something more to do with me rather than with you, but at the same time I suspect not. I have no way of measuring such distances. For myself, your work is merely promise or possibility. If pressed I do not really know. This does not mean that I talk of Titian because I am struggling to write about you, but rather I wish to find out things related to the capacity you hold within your formative gestures of becoming. Anyway you never seemed to turn away from heavy matters contained within the realities of death, eroticism, sacrifice, extreme fragmentation of the self, the scattering of limbs and blood, or anything else that might be imagined. Of course you disguise a relationship to such things with a touch, which might at times be described as whimsical, or light, and you move across surfaces and mediums with an almost foolish impatience. I know that these are the kinds of asides that someone forms in writing about the other, but I feel as though everything should touch the page with you. At this very moment someone is expecting a telephone call from me, but I cannot stop writing, so the call is suspended because you are most immediately with me. The space of writing, in such a context, should not reserve itself to discrete and distant observation but rather should demonstrate how it has been touched. I think that really this is not an essay about your work but rather the ways I have been touched since considering writing an essay about your work. Originally we had agreed that it would be a kind of collaborative dialogue and even though that has been put aside in a direct sense I still feel that what I write now is indeed a dialogue. It is strange how we might assume knowing the other. Empirically speaking we have barely passed a word to each other. Not that there is anything lacking but rather any sense of knowing comes from a region that is quite elsewhere. Sometimes it is possible to have this sense of knowing without any exchange of words. You just look and in looking exchange a sign of knowing. In such occasions you might say things such as "we will do a lot of things together" or even "I know you, somehow." So this writing springs from this apprehension of knowing that is contained within not knowing very much at all on another level. You could be Latin and Catholic as much as Greek Cypriot, radically heterogeneous or singular, a mystic or a modernist, somehow all these names could congregate around you without disturbing the course of this text.'

Untitled 7 2005-06 collage 32 x 25 cm

Untitled 6 2005-06 collage 23.8 x 22.8 cm

JARRETT MITCHELL

Born in Louisville, Kentucky, USA 1977
BFA University of Iowa
MFA California College of Arts and Crafts
Lives in Louisville
Works in Louisville, Chicago and Lee County, Iowa

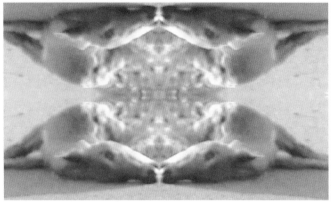

The Dawn of the Birth of the Battle of the Right to Life vs. the Law of Death 2006 video still

The Dawn of the Birth of the Battle of the Right to Life vs. the Law of Death 2006
Installation Detail

Security Is For Prisons 2003/2005
Screen Print, Courtesy of Woodward Flats

Jarrett Mitchell's drawings, sculptures, videos and installations emerge from his extensive research across a broad spectrum of contemporary and ancient cultural histories. Through the associations, reversals and repetitions, Jarrett creates a body of work which is interactive, highly politicized and concurrently cryptic and revelatory.

While many contemporary artists exhaust themselves attempting to remake or romanticize the radicalism of the 60's, Mitchell presents a model of radicalism grounded in secrecy, simplicity, self-sufficiency, and psychedelic vision. Mitchell's politics occupy a space somewhere between the Black Panthers of the 60's and the American militia movement of the 90's.

In his series "Something Is Written, Nothing Is Named", he uses Lawrence of Arabia as the archetype of the myth of the power of one man. Throughout the series Mitchell uses the Lawrence myth as a filter for the official story of Tim McVeigh, the miraculous finding on a pile of burning tower of the passport of 9-11 hi-jacker Mohamed Atta, the rise of Seabiscuit and even 2005 Kentucky Derby winner: Giacamo.

Mitchell's project for EAST 06 "The Dawn of the Birth of the Battle of the Right to Life vs. the Law of Death" an installation with painting, sculptural and video elements, focuses on the myths and realities of the American white-tailed deer. Highlighting suburban attitudes on deer as "rats with antlers" and indigenous religious beliefs of deer as gods who bring peyote and corn, Mitchell presents a multi-media cacophony where deer become collaborators of site-specific sculptures and humans become a virus more deadly and widespread than bird flu. While its view on the longevity of the culture of human animals may be pessimistic, "The Dawn of the Birth of the Battle of the Right to Life vs. the Law of Death" will emerge as Mitchell's most complete and challenging work to date.

R. Rondo, 2006

212 5/8" official score
**Top deer in Alberta
for Alberta Fish & Game
members 2003**

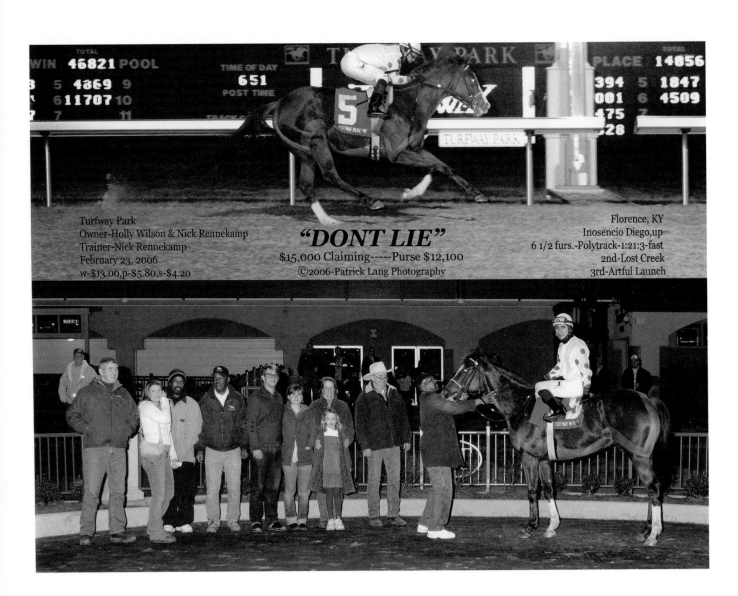

Dont Lie (Win Picture), 2006
Digital Print

Ohio State Racing Commission Groom License, 2006
Digital Print on Plastic

Something is Written, Nothing is Named (Kentucky Version), 2006
acrylic on wood, 27 x 43 cm

Lawrence of Arabia: A Biographical Inquiry

John Duncan
born 1968 Belfast
studied Gwent College of Higher Education Newport and Glasgow School Art
lives and works Belfast

My recent work examines the post-ceasefire transformation of Belfast. In the earliest work 'Boom Town' we see cleared urban spaces in which developers' hoardings give a view of the apartments, offices and civic buildings yet to be constructed, along with the lifestyles we can expect to enjoy in them. With the construction of these buildings new interfaces have been created between them and the existing communities in the city. An image from 'Trees from Germany', a series exploring these tensions, shows the lawn in front of the New Days Hotel being rolled out towards a Loyalist paramilitary mural. The most recent series 'We were here' looks at the demilitarisation that is taking place as part of the peace process. At Girdwood army barracks in North Belfast successive army regiments marked their tour of duty by painting operational banners on the internal walls of the base. During the handover to civilian contractors dismantling the base these have been painted out. The work documents these walls as part of an ongoing project registering the steady appearance of a new Belfast.

from *Trees from Germany* 2003 courtesy Belfastexposed.com C print on aluminium 50 x 60 cm
supported by The Arts Council of Northern Ireland

from *Boomtown* 2000- C print on aluminium size 20 x 25cm each

from *We were here* 2006 C print on aluminium size variable

from *We were here* 2006 C print on aluminium size variable

John Goodwin
born 1963 Birmingham
studied Coventry University and Manchester Metropolitan
lives and works Plymouth

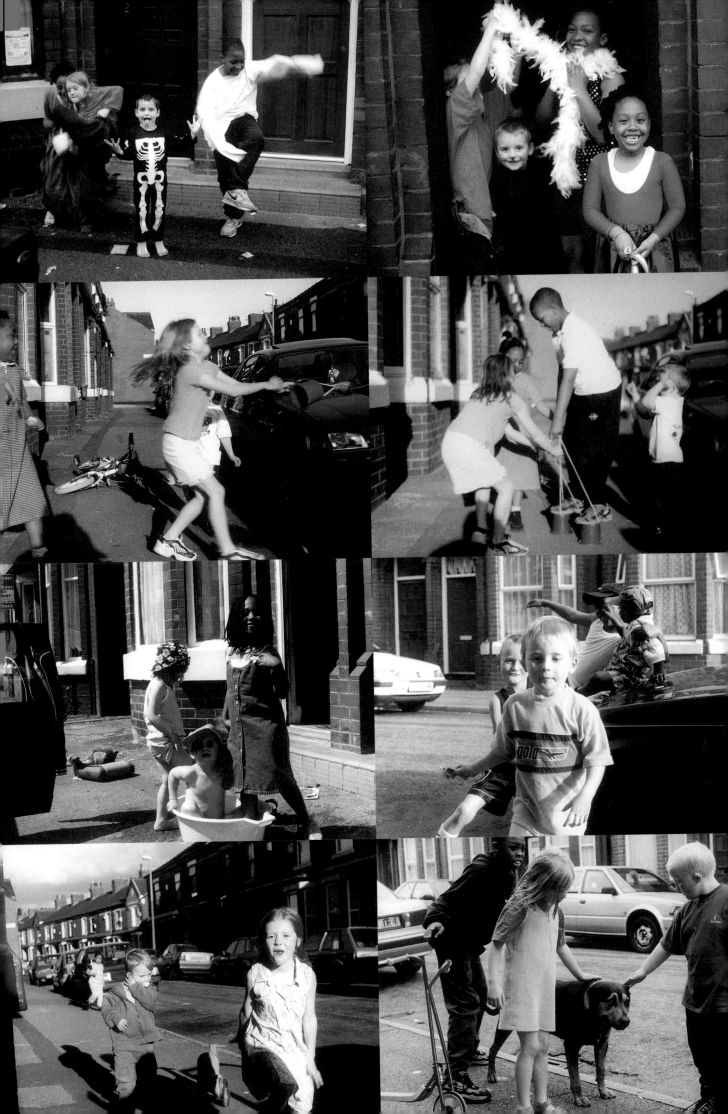

Kate Williams
born 1971 Builth Wells Powys Wales
studied Wolverhampton University
studied with Keith Cummings
lives and works London
www.katewilliams.org

John Lloyd
born 1965 Wells
studied Cambridge University
lives and works London

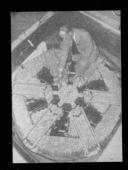

Whisky an' biscad
death of the atom

John O'Groat Journal

UKAEA taken to task by pollution agency

Terrier rescued after cliff plunge

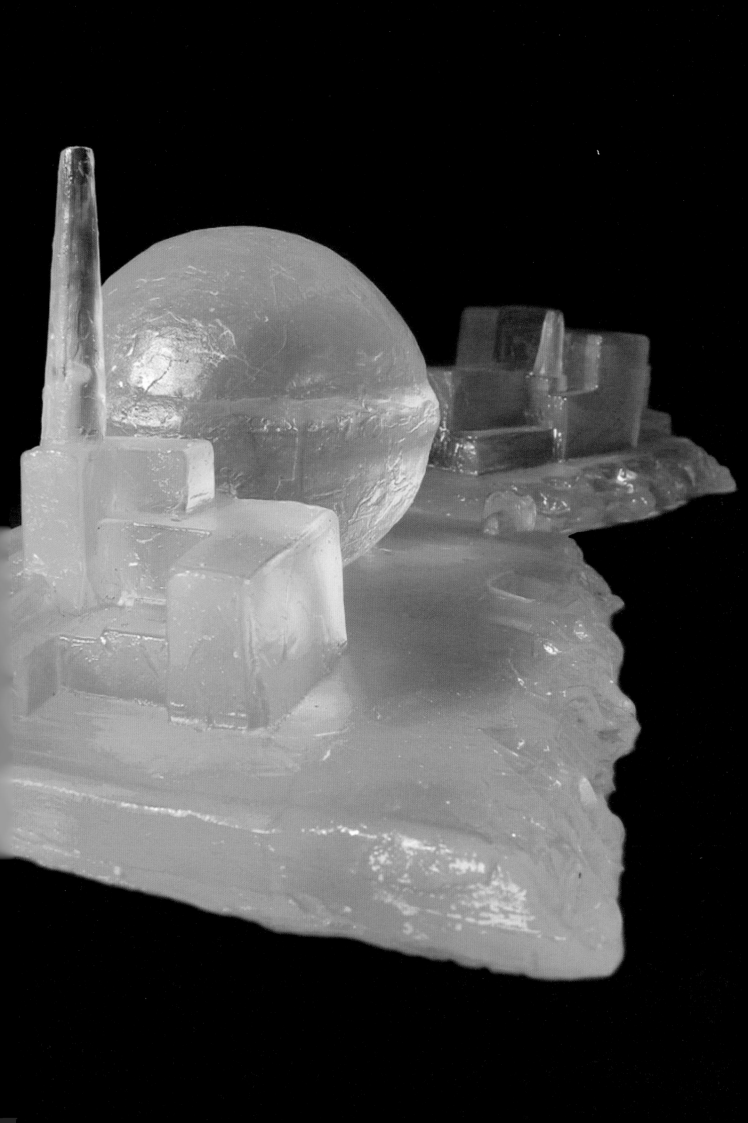

Keith Farquhar
born 1969 Edinburgh
studied Edinburgh College of Art and Goldsmiths College London
lives and works Edinburgh
represented by Anthony Reynolds Gallery
www.keithfarquhar.co.uk

The Hoxton Fin

It was when I was at Goldsmiths in 1995-96 doing an M.A. under Gerard Hemsworth and Simon Linke (we got to have Michael Craig Martin for a few months) that I invented the Hoxton Fin.

I was living in Deptford with Chloe, the exotic daughter of a *Zero Group* flamethrower painter of the late sixties. We were on the same course and she had a spare room in one of those 1930s brick built council flats that are beautifully tiled inside. She would do the hoovering naked with big high heels on and I'd come home with a little heroin and try to prolong this. The first time we got it on was after a Saatchi opening. We had just been kicked out of the Colony Rooms for lewd behaviour – it seems we couldn't keep our hands off each other. She propositioned that if I paid the taxi to the Hilton then she would pay for the room. And so we arrived and it wasn't just a room but a whole suite.

I remember that we didn't have full sex. We had a bath together, then we probably fell asleep. In the morning she dressed in her burgundy P.V.C. skintights and I licked them all over as if they were a second skin. She paid by credit card and I saw that the bill was for two hundred and fifty pounds.

So we're back south of the river and I've probably been swimming in the local pool – taking time out from the breaststroke to watch the disabled black kids supervised in the water; or looking in the window of the Jewish tailor next door at the photos of all the celebrities whom he had been making suits for Vic Reeves, Chris Evans, probably Jarvis Cocker. Anyway, I'm walking along Deptford High Street towards college, having just come out of the barber with a bad haircut. (My mother had always cut my hair to my specifications- "Don't let anyone notice I've had a haircut" I'd warn - how can you tell a barber that?) The thing is I'd already been home and played about with it in the mirror. I'd seen a documentary called *Punks in Prague* where there were guys coming out of communism saying things like - "*I used to work in the factory making the Skoda but now I am punk*" or "*I have the two kid and the wife and I work making the auto for Skoda but now I am punk*".

So I organized my hair into the bad mohawk with the sides not really shaved off that they had on the programme and when I arrived at my group seminar everyone seemed to love it.

A few months of wearing this style around London raised a few eyebrows before I found myself at another Saatchi opening. (By this time I had moved on to the side parting.) Two young trendies with David Beckham-to-be haircuts were looking over the room at me. I could see one was gesturing to the other - "That's the guy who had the original mohawk".

It was at this moment, I now realise, that I had invented the Hoxton Fin.

Nice pair of trainers, shoes, jeans and a top 2005
Hooded sweatshirts, jeans, trainers, shoes, denim and accompanying soundtrack
Installed at Inverleith House Edinburgh November 2005

Atomised 2005 Hooded sweatshirts, jeans and aluminium
Installed at Nyehaus New York September 2005

Kevin Hutcheson
born 1971 Glasgow
studied Duncan of Jordanstone College of Art & Design Dundee
and Chelsea College of Art & Design London
lives and works Glasgow

European Canon 2004 magazine cuttings and card on paper 25 x 17.5 cm

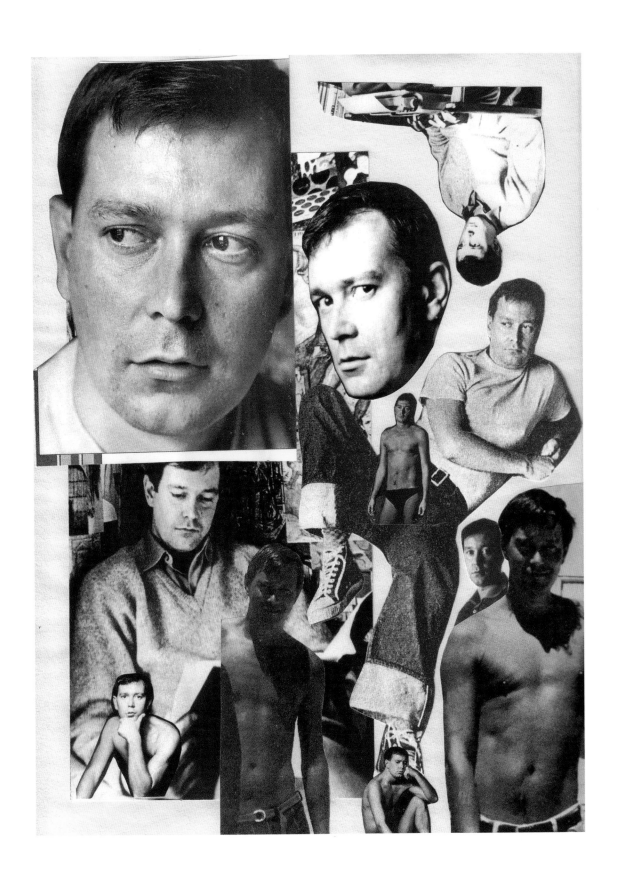

Looted 2004 magazine cuttings on paper 32 x 22 cm

The Dreaming 2005 magazine cutting on magazine page 30 x 22 cm

The Dreaming(2) 2005 watercolour and card on magazine cutting 18 x 12 cm

Mark Boulos
born 1975 USA
studied Swarthmore College Philadelphia National Film and Television School London
lives and works London

And the truth shall make you free
Mark Boulos by Ossian Ward

In Mark Boulos's first film, *Self-Defense* of 2001, a young Muslim named Ibrahim Ibrahim Muhammad from Mauritania who lives in Brooklyn, New York tells the camera how he travelled to Afghanistan at the age of 14 or 15 to be trained by the Taliban. This self-confessed *jihadi* goes on to rail against the evils of his adopted country and emote his disenfranchisement. He uses didactic and apocalyptic language – "crush", "kill", "destroy", "burn" – clearly the textbook vocabulary of an extremist. As we listen to this man's increasingly bold statements, it becomes clear that while he has certainly been indoctrinated, we too are being slowly indoctrinated by his radical beliefs because, unlike a normal documentary film, we are offered no opposing view, no journalistic balancing act. Ironically, Ibrahim challenges *our* acquiescent acceptance of reality when he says, "People don't think, people are programmed, whatever they see, hear or listen… they accept anything, everything." At the very end of the film we have further reason to question the narrator's veracity when he claims not to know where Al Qaeda are based. He smiles mischievously, perhaps because he really knows nothing at all, or perhaps because as Susan Sontag once said, "Lying is the most simple form of self-defense".

As Boulos was trained at the National Film and Television School, there is a temptation to view his work with the same dispassionate eye that we reserve for factual documentaries. This aura of authenticity is reinforced by his use of the documentary medium's trademark techniques, such as interviews, handheld digital camerawork, and reference to political events.

However, Boulos himself is complicit in fuelling the anti-US diatribe in *Self-Defense*, given that he is interviewer, director and by association, author of the whole scenario. Is he in fact sympathetic to this apologist of September 11 because, despite being American by birth, he is Arabic by descent? To entertain such a rash conclusion is to inhabit the very realm of conspiracy theory that informs so many post-9/11 responses and would be to disregard the visual poignancy of his own photographs of the fall of the Twin Towers, which are intercut with the young guerrilla's proclamations on the benefits of war. This contradictory combination of sound and image short-circuits the consensus of Western outrage, leaving us with a mixture of the disinformation

of an Islamic fundamentalist and the ambiguity of a potentially unreliable director, who is neither sceptic nor supporter, and who is an artist rather than an impartial journalist.

Another militant Muslim, Britain's highest profile 'enemy within', Abu Hamza, is the subject of *Jerusalem*, a three-minute work by Boulos of 2003. The hook-handed, firebrand imam is depicted preaching in the street outside the Finsbury Park Mosque and is absurdly juxtaposed with an Arabic translation of William Blake's famous hymn *Jerusalem* and the sexually provocative gyrations of a belly dancer. Abu Hamza's speech reflects the rabble-rousing tone of Blake's original, in which he advocated both a "mental fight" and the use of sword, bows, arrows and spears in a crusade for the creation of a new Jerusalem in Britain – an ironic evocation of the revolutionary language that fuels jihad. Although the hegemony of the Church of England has been usurped by the secular power of government and the "dark satanic mills" of industrialisation replaced by today's rampant capitalism, Blake's plea that the new Jerusalem should be built by prophets rather than and profiteers is still relevant. However, Boulos complicates this choice through his use of the politically problematic figure of Abu Hamza, who can be perceived as both symbol of oppression and hatred.

The paradoxical nature of religious faith as well as its transcendental beauty is explored in a longer work, *The Gates of Damascus*, 2005. It follows housewife and mother, Myrna Nazzour, whose vision of the Virgin Mary and subsequent, dramatic visitations from Jesus have turned her ancient Christian enclave in Syria's Muslim capital into a place of pilgrimage. Boulos filmed her Easter Week reliving of the Passion of Christ in which she displays stigmata wounds, oozes oil from her face and hands, and writhes in ecstasy before revealing a message from Jesus. Again, the absence of voiceover means the viewer is left to navigate this unusual terrain alone, as you would a novel or even scripture. The film both stimulates and relies on this interaction for its meaning.

Once in a while Boulos implies his subject's vicarious 'divinity'; once by briefly dwelling on her profile as though she were the Virgin receiving the message in a fresco by Giotto and on another occasion by wielding the camera aloft as if observing her direct from heaven. These saintly shots are quickly demystified either by the acoustical intrusion of a car horn from outside or by the visual intrusion of another film crew looming over her bed – revealing the event to be just as much a modern day media circus as it is a spiritual séance. This ambivalence to the main character could also extend to the Christ she imitates – were the miracles of Jesus any more convincing to behold, any less a product of the crowd's expectation?

The hushed climax is Myrna's utterance of a communiqué, purportedly straight from Jesus himself: "…hold the East in your hearts. You are its radiance in a world seduced by materialism, sensuality and fame… Do not allow your will, your freedom and your faith in this Orient to be taken away from you." In an 'earthing' epilogue, we witness Myrna having her hair done in a classy salon before going shopping with her daughter Myriam, a display of sensuality and femininity that was conspicuously absent during her psychic episode.

In *The Gates of Damascus*, as in *Jerusalem* and *Self-Defense*, the ambiguities and illusions of religious faith are also revealed to be inherent in the documentary medium. With our faith in film's empiricism eroded, we can only hope that "truth declares itself in a structure of fiction", as Derrida said, and that Boulos is objectively analysing and questioning religion and faith, rather than promoting or persuading us of some hidden agenda. Perhaps more artists should learn to be consummate realists before attempting fiction or artifice, although in the work of Boulos the dividing line between the real and the imaginary has been blurred indefinitely.

For EAST, Boulos is presenting a new work, *The Word was God*. He shot it in the last Christian village in Syria where Aramaic is still spoken, as well as in a Pentecostal Church in Dalston, East London. It was made possible by grants from the Arts Council of England and the British Documentary Film Foundation.

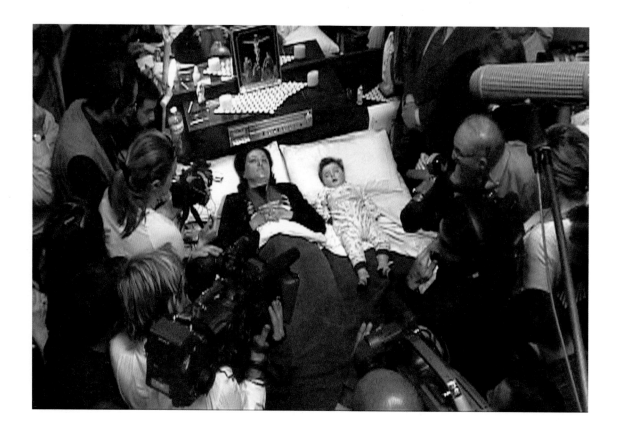

Jerusalem 2003
The Gates of Damascus 2005

The Word was God 2006

Masayuki Suzuki
born 1974 Hamamatu Japan
studied Tokyo Zokei University and City & Guilds London
lives and works London

Majestic Boy

Majestic Boy

Majestic Boy

THE FEDERATION OF MASTER ORGAN BUILDERS

THE NATIONAL UNION OF MUSICAL INSTRUMENT MAKERS

"THE ORGAN OF TRADITION"

We respectfully call your attention to the enclosed Brochure in which is presented the case for the organ of tradition as the most suitable type of musical instrument for use in public worship, and especially invite you to read the article contributed by the Revd. Noel A. Bonavia-Hunt as a fair and well reasoned argument from the worshipper's point of view.

No one can fail to admire the ingenuity that has succeeded in producing "electronic" instruments and doubtless further improvements are to be anticipated. But the question at issue is very largely this:- whether the loud speaker as a source of musical tone is worthy in our places of worship, and whether the ousting of the organ of historic tradition - the product of many centuries - in favour of its electronic imitation is a step in the right direction.

The ultimate responsibility lies with those in whom is vested the power of choice and it is felt that at least they would desire to be equipped with such knowledge of the subject as will enable them to exercise their privilege of selection in the best interests of the religious community.

It is only natural that in some quarters there should be a tendency in the direction of giving a trial to modern inventions, but in this case it is generally agreed among organists and musicians that as yet nothing can replace the organ of tradition in its capacity to create a reverent and devotional atmosphere in God's House.

In cases where lack of space for a pipe organ or other con- siderations make the installation of an electronic instrument appear to be inevitable it should be noted that British made instruments of that type are available.

The Brochure is therefore commended for consideration and study in the hope that it may prove to be both interesting and helpful.

For and on behalf of
THE FEDERATION OF MASTER ORGAN BUILDERS

Secretary: 5, Coleman Street,
London, E.C.2.

THE NATIONAL UNION OF MUSICAL INSTRUMENT MAKERS

Secretary: 308, Gray's Inn Road,
London, W.C.1.

April, 1939.

Matt Stokes
born 1973 Penzance Cornwall
studied Newcastle University
lives and works Newcastle upon Tyne

Sacred Selections
(Experimental Transcriptions Of Underground Music)

At first glance, the idea of transcribing what could be considered Lo-Art forms of music for the pipe organ seems absurd. Is not the organ one of the oldest instruments in Western music? Is it not the privy of Johann Sebastian Bach, Henry Purcell and other such figureheads of our revered Classical tradition? Did not Olivier Messiaen, one of the giants of 20th Century composition devote his religious life to playing the organ at the Church Of The Holy Trinity in Paris, every day for nearly sixty years? Why then transcribe forms of ephemeral music for what has always been perceived as a mainstay of Western culture?

But as always the deeper one delves into something the more contradictions and revelations are unearthed. Olivier Messiaen, though a staunch conservative in spiritual terms, was one of the chief architects of the musical Year Zero which occurred at Darmstadt in Germany in 1950. It was Messiaen's revolutionary grasp of sound that birthed whole oceans of music in the forms of Total Serialism, 'synaesthetic' or hallucinatory music, electronic music and a greater interest in timbral music that led to the rise of Ambient in the late 20th Century. Even the most cursory of glances across the landscape of 20th Century music reveals the organ as a key instrument in the development of modern sound.

When The Beatles were shaping history in Abbey Road, the revolving Leslie Speaker Cabinet of a Hammond organ became a vital tool in 'psychedelicising' their music. Brian Wilson's bass organ vamping became a hallmark of the complex symphonic pop melodies of The Beach Boys. When The Doors became the biggest band in America in 1967, their music (especially the hit *Light My Fire*) was fuelled by Ray Manzarek's Bach-like double-organ solos. The Grateful Dead's high-watermark album from 1969, *Live/Dead*, was characterised by Tom Constanten's filigreed organ rising through a dense forest of psychedelic guitars. In fact psychedelia, a form of rock inspired by LSD, was characterised by an organ solo somewhere in the mix on both sides of the Atlantic during the 1960s. From The Electric Prunes to Pink Floyd the organ was ubiquitous in the sonic landscape. Led Zeppelin's awesome debut album from 1969 contains a stirring church organ solo from John-Paul Jones, himself an accomplished organist and arranger. Even Jazz pianist Keith Jarrett switched to the organ in 1976 when he wanted to expand his repertoire, this time for the double album

Hymns/Spheres where he used partial openings of the organ stops at a Benedictine Abbey to produce new tonalities within organ improvisation.

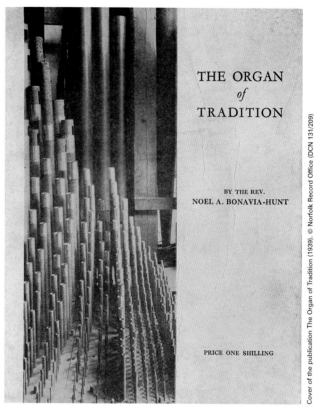

Cover of the publication The Organ of Tradition (1939). © Norfolk Record Office (DCN 131/209)

So those of you who come to hear the musical genres of Northern Soul, Happy Hardcore and Black Metal, and reel in disbelief at the idea of their transcription for the pipe organ should think again. The concept came from Matt Stokes, following a meeting with the Tayside Organists, and the Dundee City Organist. Their conversations led him to the Episcopal Church of St Salvador's and a revelation that the halls of the church were once used to host Northern Soul nights in the 1970s. As a result, he developed notions of marrying location and Soul music through the use of the pipe organ. Not as fanciful an idea as it sounds given that the roots of Northern Soul are in the Church and Gospel music.

Stokes also considered the historical aspects of the organ as both a secular and sacred instrument, and then expanded the idea to encompass other types of non-mainstream music that have connections to communities and places in Northern Britain. With Happy Hardcore he saw a strong association between Scotland and this style of epic Dance music. During the 1980s/90s the first rush of House Music diversified into dozens of sub-genres. In Southern England, in particular, the process birthed new sonic forms such as Jungle or Drum & Bass, an amalgamation of Acid House and black forms of music such as of Reggae and Hip-Hop. In contrast, the North held onto the more euphoric roots of Acid House, as embodied through the naive and often simplistic constructions of Happy Hardcore music.

But then what has Black Metal got to do with either churches or the organ other than connotations of dark environs, rituals and the night? During his research, Stokes also encountered communities into various forms of extreme Heavy Metal music including Thrash, Doom and Black Metal - a form closely connected with sub-genres such as Occult and Death Metal. However, what characterises Black Metal music is its use of Satanic lyrics and imagery, which in part inspired Stokes to utilise this form in the recitals, as "it is the antithesis of what would usually be played on a pipe organ."

Manipulated illustration from the cover of 'Modern Transcriptions for the Organ No.16' (C.1930)

So, between the 8th July and 19th August 2006, Norwich will host a series of pipe organ recitals under the banner of *Sacred Selections*: at an English Gothic Anglican church, a busy United Reformed church, a civic concert hall, and even some performed on a small two-manual and pedal organ sited in Norwich Gallery. A common thread between the chosen musical genres is the quality of immersion, of somehow losing oneself in the sound, of being elevated (in the case of Happy Hardcore) or being viscerally charged by the intensities and rhythms of the music, (as with Black Metal or Northern Soul). Another connection is that these genres lie on the periphery of what is considered the mainstream - as being somehow radical in nature. And in the mid 1800s the introduction of pipe organs into somber settings like Scottish Presbyterian churches seemed like a radical, even avant-garde ideal. But given the nature of the source music - released on rare 45rpm records, 12-inch records and obscure albums, how was it possible to transcribe it for the organ?

In consideration of Northern Soul recordings (often scratchy vinyl in swing rhythms produced on-the-fly in backstreet studios with classically untrained vocalists), transcription was achieved "with great difficulty" according to Andrew Macintosh who carried out the painstaking work in this area. If one then thinks about the translation of Black Metal to the organ, and the likes of music by Cradle Of Filth and Bathory (a Swedish band named after the infamous 17th Century Transylvanian Countess who was a real-life vampire!), the idea seems implausible. But, in terms of attack and volume the concept has its own logic which stands up historically. During the 20th Century the expansion of sound has been

characterised by a greater emphasis on timbre either live or in the studio. Certainly, Heavy Metal Rock as birthed by Led Zeppelin was a triumph of precision timing, ferocious unison attack on drums/bass/guitar and an understanding of Jimmy Page's favourite term "light and shade" in both the composition and recording processes. Thus Black Metal characterises itself by taking the classic template of Led Zeppelin and pushing it to extremes of attack and volume in the guitar and vocal departments. This facet makes transcription for organ doubly complex as an organ does not respond to those extremes. Hence when playing this music the organ has to be pushed to its limits.

With its array of keyboards, setter buttons, stops, couplers and foot pedals the piped church organ is not something to be taken lightly. The idea of transcribing vocal Soul or Metal guitar music to the instrument seems exceptionally difficult, but you are still dealing with structured forms. When it comes to House music, particularly the ecstatic form known as Rave, you are dealing with whooshes of sound and electronic crescendos originally designed to imbue a transcendent emotion closely allied to the chemical effects of the drug Ecstasy. In transcribing the selected tracks for the organ, the idea was to keep the basic chordal and melodic structures combined with new textures more in common with 20th Century harmonic thinking. Basically holding onto the tune and riffs, and not attempting to replicate the complex and often erratic properties of early drum machines and samplers.

A superficial view of *Sacred Selections* is that it's a fanciful even experimental idea that has little or no connection with 'real' music, whatever that is supposed to be. The 20th Century, with its over-arching spirit of innovation shows that nothing in music is superficial, but comes from a long history of ground-breaking events. When Karlheinz Stockhausen debuted *Gesang Der Junglinge (Song Of The Youths)* in Koln in 1956 he caused uproar because instead of an orchestra on stage there were speakers playing an electronic mass that the composer had spent six months splicing onto tape. Many felt it was the death of music, but fifty years on we are still feeling the waves of his electronic revolution. In a way the transcription of underground music for the pipe organ continues that spirit of innovation, a spirit that is essential if music is to remain a vital force in all our lives.

© Mark Prendergast 2006

This is an edited version of an essay commissioned by Locus+

- SACRED - SELECTIONS

A SERIES OF PIPE ORGAN RECITALS FEATURING EXPERIMENTAL TRANSCRIPTIONS OF UNDERGROUND MUSIC

- Northern Soul -

St Peter Mancroft Church, Millennium Plain, Norwich
FRIDAY 21ST JULY 2006, AT 8 O'CLOCK

- Happy Hardcore -

United Reformed Church, Princes Street, Norwich
FRIDAY 4TH AUGUST 2006, AT 8 O'CLOCK

Music selected by: DJ Sy (Quosh Records)
Transcribed for the organ by: John Riley (St Paul's & St George's Episcopal Church, Edinburgh)

- Black Metal -

St Andrew's Hall, St Andrew's Plain, Norwich
FRIDAY 11TH AUGUST 2006, AT 8 O'CLOCK

Music selected by: Bruno Frenguelli and Grim Reality
Transcribed for the organ by: Andrew Macintosh (Royal College of Organists)

ADMISSION TO THE EVENTS IS FREE

Nate Harrison,
born 1972 Eugene Oregon American
studied University of Michigan and California Institute of the Arts
lives and works Los Angeles

Can I Get An Amen? Is an audio installation including a spoken word recording on an acetate 'test pressing', played on a conventional turntable, that recounts a historical critical perspective of perhaps the most sampled drumbeat in the history of recorded music, the Amen Break. The Amen Break is heard everywhere in popular culture, from underground electronic music to ESPN to commercials for Visa, yet its story is relatively unknown. The recording begins with the pop track Amen Brother by the 60's soul band The Winstons, and then traces the transformation of the drum solo in the middle of the song from its original context as part of an ordinary 'B' side vinyl single into its use as a key aural ingredient in contemporary cultural expression as well as commerce. The subtext in the recording revolves around a seeming paradox introduced through the story: the exponential growth of digital tools over the past decade has allowed for increasing efficiency and transparency in appropriation strategies in creative production, even while the growing global legal system, often influenced by corporate agendas, enacts legislation that problematizes those very strategies. In turn, this brings into scrutiny the techno-utopian notion that 'information wants to be free' – it questions its effectiveness as a democratizing and thus utopian social agent. To what extent does information being free lead to a levelling of the 'knowledge playing field', and to what extent does information being free actually further restrict access to knowledge by allowing those with money and resources to manipulate information for the benefit of a select minority? These questions are touched upon through a history of the Amen Break and its relation to current copyright law.

Nate Harrison

33 1/3 RPM
17:46
3_ of 10, ed. 1

"Can I Get An Amen"

www.nstprojects.org

Can I Get An Amen? 2004
Recording on acetate, turntable, loudspeakers, paper documents
Total run time 17 minutes 46 seconds

Rebecca Birch
born 1978 Birmingham
studied UCE Birmingham Goldsmiths and the Slade
lives and works London

NORTH SEA

NORWICH

HAPPISBURGH

CAMBRIDGE

POTENTIAL COASTLINE

NORTH SEA

LONDON

based upon a map produced by The Environment Agency
as published in *East Anglian Daily Times* 1999

Because the erosion happens so slowly it creeps up on you without you noticing, if it all went overnight, if fifty feet went overnight, you know, there'd be a hue and a cry, but when just a little bit goes, I mean my garden in the last two years has probably lost, inch by inch, about two feet. And so it creeps up on you and you don't notice it too much. So there was a lot more land there but it wasn't really.. . because it's near the cliff edge it wasn't really productive like it was further back. The grass gets salty. And where the house is now is lovely because you can see right along the beach, but if anymore dropped away I don't think my wife would be very happy.

And you, you know, you lose a ramp, and a certain amount of cliff has gone, and you lose a ramp, and you've got to start all over again and you think to yourself, 'cor, you know, what a ruddy turn out all this is', and you start again, and you think, well, you know, optimistically that mighty not happen for another 10 years or so, but it does, it might be shorter, it might be longer, but it happens again, and it happens again and again and that's how it's always going to be, with different time spans in between.

Well I don't know, I mean that shingle must have come from somewhere.

Yeah, lovely, and it's good, but it won't last.

Well who's to know? I've never known that much shingle down here and I've been fishing with you, I mean I've been fishing down here for years and I've never known it shingle like there is now. It'll slow it down.

But in one enormous blow with the tide right that's gone, don't matter how much is there, that's gone, and it'll happen, and it'll happen again.

It was wonderful up there. There were sea views all around and there was always something happening, you know. Big ships, all through the night. And I had my telescope up in the roof. Could see the men working out on the oil rigs, crystal clear, it was.

We used to sleep in the front porch that was the furthest inland, you know, and the dogs slept there and I knew if anything happened they'd wake me.

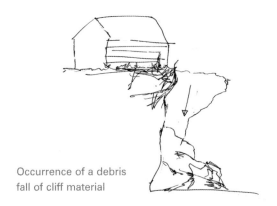

Occurrence of a debris
fall of cliff material

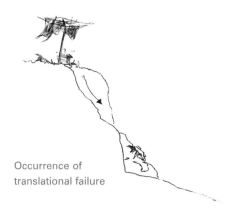

Occurrence of
translational failure

Well I started to worry when the gardens began to fall…97 really.

They suddenly collapsed everywhere. It's worrying to hear that at the moment some experts are saying that no, no, no, we're quite wrong, it's only going at less than one and a half metres a year when we know from our own measurements- this house that we're passing now, they lost- when he has lost almost 3 metres in the last 3 months. And she's lost in total about 60 metres of land in two and a half years. So it's incredibly quickly.

So these houses are all…?

All doomed, yes.

All these here are doomed.

Peace and tranquillity I suppose, that's the thing I like. It's delightful, things move slowly, delightful. And it's such a very friendly village, there's a tremendous amount going on here, we have a village hall, and it is difficult booking a room in the village hall because there are so many things going on there. It's extraordinary.

Now, this man, he has lived here for many, many years, he's 84 I think now and he's hysteric, quite clearly. His caravan was right on the edge until a few months ago, we were talking to him, saying 'for heaven's sake, please move your caravan' and he said, 'oh, I shall know when it's going, don't worry'. And he said, 'at my age, I don't care if I go over with it'. Eventually we persuaded him to move it from there to bring it over here, so he's got a few more feet yet, but it won't be long.

Come and talk to Mr Thomas, he's a delightful man.

Hello!

Mr Thomas!

I think he's at home, the car's there.

The car's here and the door's open.

Yep, I think he'll be here. Well perhaps he's gardening.

Is he in the greenhouse?

No, he's not there. I don't think I'd dare to go into that greenhouse, it's so near the edge. See what a magnificent view he's got, it's gorgeous. Looking out over the sea like that! I should think it was grim the last few days when we had those storms.

I'm sure he wouldn't mind my taking you to the edge, come, come.

You've certainly come on a nice day. Gorgeous isn't it?

Now you see how high the garden was before, right up at the top. It sank down what, 30, 40 feet perhaps. And it will just go on crumbling right down to the edge and disappear soon. His house stood out here, extraordinary, he had roughly a hundred yards from where he is now. Well, it cracked, you could see that, you know, he'd lost a lot of land, and then when it approached the house the house itself cracked, and then his house tipped, it was quite interesting it tipped backwards towards the sea, and he still went on living there, till finally of course it was obvious he could hardly get into the house, the doors weren't opening and that sort of thing and he got a caravan. He's a tough character.

Oh! Mr Thomas! Forgive me for charging in, I'm always charging in on you.

You keep measuring it don't you?

Oh, yes, we measure and measure. You know they're saying that it will go at a rate of not less than one and a half metres a year for next hundred years, the experts are saying.

But I used to reckon it would go at about a foot a year, the last fifty years or so, so that is just weathering more than anything, it weathers.

Yes. But every so often we get these tremendous falls, don't we?

Well yes, yes, but then nothing happens for years sort of thing, you know.

I mean I used to get, when it was routine, two or three yards would go, then nothing for ten years really. I remember I used to play with the dog in the evening and I threw a ball once and the bloomin' dog disappeared, of course during the day a chunk had gone. It hadn't gone far, he'd only gone down to two or three feet, or two or three yards, but he was a bit surprised.

And again, there was a footpath beyond that, a wood beyond that, which we had a little seat in, you know. So it's about a hundred yards have gone.

Fantastic isn't it?

But it's happened though in the last decade sort of thing.

I like the look of your dog now you've trimmed him.

Different dog look isn't she? Yes she sunbaths now, wouldn't dare do that before.

You're still using your greenhouse then?

Half of it, yes. I've got tomatoes in there and that sort of thing growing. But that's only temporary, it's not going to last long I shouldn't think.

It's teetering on the brink.

Yes it is, that side, but the side nearest the garage, that's alright at the moment. Like I say, there's nothing you can do about it, so why worry about it?

ST. GEORGE'S ESTATE RESIDENTS

AN END TO CULTURE ASSAULTS

CARNIVAL OF COMMUNITY

THE NEW MURAL

A NEW SACRIFICE A NEW COMMUNITY

LET YOUR BODY FEED OUR CULTURE

Murder Considered as a Fine Art
(The Ritualised Death of the International Mural Artist)

Having found ourselves assaulted by a wretched 'art', namely the appearance on the St. George's Estate, Shadwell, East London of a mural 200 metres in length, dramatic recourse has been planned for not only this but other incidences of state sanctioned violence.

The first of a series of televised events at St. George's commences on the mid-summer's solstice evening and will include opportunities for spontaneous resident participation. Under a blood red Waterloo Sunset the proceedings will unfold thus:

The artist / commissioner / curator / project manager will be bathed, anointed with oils, dressed in a fine suit of clothes and served by the residents of the estate with a meal exquisitely prepared and lasting 12 hours.

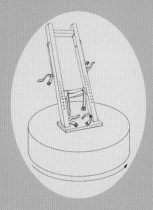

After a night sleeping in the Temple erected on the Estate Green and guarded by resident 'wardens', the sacrifice will rise and spend the day being presented by the Executioner to the crowd consisting of residents, other artists / commissioners and members of the braying public invited to compete in their cursing of the pilloried subject.

Come early evening he / she will be tortured with a degree of prejudice understood after consultation with residents, to be in accordance with his / her crime (a.k.a mural

intervention, workshop) and subject to the sacrificial lamb's consent. The method of execution will be dependent on the wishes of the public and the sacrifice. The method can range from hanging, garroting, being smote with a mutton bone; the list is endless but dependent on resident consultation.

The cadaver will then be staked through the heart and placed upon a truck fitted with a revolving stage and frame that will present the gouting corpse at a 45 degree angle to the braying mob as the float circumnavigates the estate.

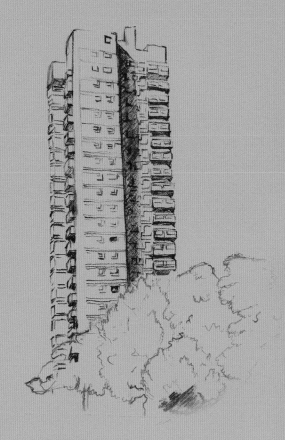

The Procession will commence along The Highway, passing News International's Headquarters, go north up Cannon Street Road and then west along Cable Street before repeating this circuit to return to the civil engineered abyss at the corner of Cable Street and Cannon Street Road.

At the specially crafted shaft designed to receive a limitless number of sacrifices, and beneath the garland of joy suspended between the buildings, the cadaver will be hurled into this sucking chasm prompting a chorus of ecstatic cries from the attending crowd and echoed by the bellow of audiences viewing the event on television at home. It is envisaged that demand will be so great for this facility that barely a day will go by without the abyss being gorged with the flesh of those seeking atonement. This excavated gullet is designed to feed the foundations of the estate providing in turn a life force that will require replenishing at an exponential rate. The thirst of this Brutalist designed set of buildings will be like that of a jet engine sucking air and fuel into its lungs setting alight the souls of its residents; transforming them into raging incandescent flames of being.

St. George's Estate, The LCC Architecture Office & Emmanuel Swedenborg:

St. George's Estate is an early 1960s London County Council (LCC) designed estate of approximately 2,000 residents, approximately 1,800 of which are Syhleti speaking Bangladeshi. The buildings are mixed elevation, medium density with open green spaces. The east side of the estate faces Nicolas Hawksmoor's Church St. George's in the East and a row of 18th Century town houses. Cable Street and the heavily fortified News International print works are respectively north and south of the estate. The same architect's office was responsible for the design of the Hayward Gallery and the estate uses aspects of a 'Brutalist' school of Modernism that the Hayward has become synonymous with.

The design is distinct from the more humanist school of modernism adopted by parts of the same LCC office that were responsible for the Alton East Estate in Roehampton, for example. English Heritage and DOCOMOMO (the international working party for documentation and conservation of buildings, sites and neighbourhoods of the modern movement) have voiced support for the St.George's Estate buildings calling for any improvements to be sympathetic to its original scheme and noting that the estate's downfall in the last 25 years has been mainly due to a lack of maintenance and care by the local authority.

The eighteenth-century philosopher, scientist and Christian theologian Emmanuel Swedenborg arrived in London in 1744 after allegedly receiving divine guidance to publish in the city. He stayed with a member of the local Moravian community, John Paul Brockmer, at a house on the site now occupied by the medium rise block of 69 flats called Brockmer House. Swedenborg left in July of the same year shortly after having a vision that according to Brockmer caused him to foam at the mouth, strip naked, repair to a place called the Gulley-Hole and roll in deep mud, throwing his money to the crowd whilst declaring himself to be 'the messiah...come to be crucified by the Jews.'

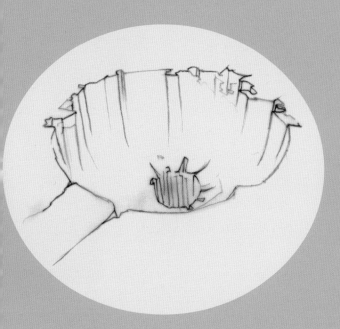

St. George's will become a national fairground of joy where cultural workers and cultural recidivist of all kinds will have the opportunity to feed the public, allowing their bodies to become the site(s) and feast for a 'coming together', a letting of blood and cleansing of their previous pernicious cultural mugging.

Subsequent architectural modifications to the buildings on the estate will accommodate aerial viewing platforms and towers for burning pyres that will announce the advent and duration of each new carnival. The pilot event will take place on mid-summer's night but the envisaged demand and throughput will take on quasi industrial proportions demanding that this become an all weather event and facility.

Roman Vasseur born 1967 London
Resident
St. George's Estate
Shadwell, East London.

The Ratcliffe Highway Murders & Thomas de Quincey:

On the evening of the 7 December, 1811 an entire family including a baby were brutally murdered at a Draper's shop in St.George's Street adjoining Ratcliffe Highway, now known simply as The Highway (a main road that leads from Tower Hill to Limehouse). Local anger at the crimes and the posting of £500 reward resulted in the mob arresting a man named John Williams who may have committed the subsequent murder of a pub landlady. Williams escaped execution outside Newgate Gaol by hanging himself in his cell thereby denying a public the retribution it demanded. The then Home Secretary instructed that the body be publicly paraded past the crime-scenes and buried at a crossroads in the manner reserved for suicides. 10,000 people lined the route and

watched the burial. In August 1886 a gas company discovered the skeleton of John Williams (with a stake driven through it) during the excavation of a trench. It was six feet below the surface of the road where Cannon Street Road and Cable Street cross.

For a short period in 1818 Thomas de Quincey (author of Confessions of an English Opium-Eater) was editor of Westmorland Gazette and demonstrated a taste for descriptions of violent murder by replacing the news with collections of lurid stories from across the country; a fascination which seemed in contrast to his gentle character. De Quincy made Williams his prize practitioner in the development of

his notion of connoisseurship or dilettantism in murder; i.e. a class of artist/murderer that no other could match. De Quincey developed a mock-morality where issues are ingeniously reversed, as in the passage from the second paper on 'Murder Considered as One of the Fine Arts' (Masson, vol. xiii, p. 56)

'If once a man indulges himself in murder, very soon he comes to think little of robbing; and from robbing he comes next to drinking and Sabbath-breaking, and from that to incivility and procrastination. Once begun upon his downward path, you never know where you are to stop. Many a man has dated his ruin from some murder or other that perhaps he thought little of at the time.'

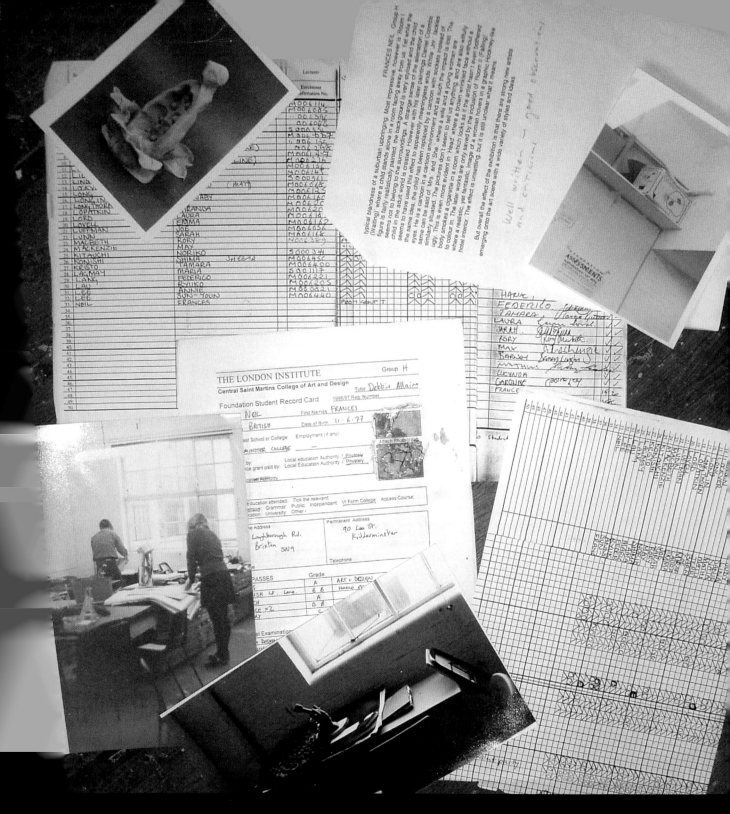

piece of proper artwork I was involved with was Frances Neil, a fake foundation student at Central St. Martin's invented by myself
Lord. We broke into the college office, enrolled her, forged her attendance sheets and watched as she became officially absorbed
lege burocracy. From that moment on, she was marked as absent, so we started the rumour amongst the students that she had been
for having a relationship with a tutor, which spread quickly, adding a bit of weight to her admin existance . Her first essay got a
mark. As assessment approached, we decided to produce a portfolio for her. Her entire collection of work was put together in 3
work we found in college bins, and from getting our respective flatmates (mostly non-artists) to help us churn out the remaining
eveloped a leaning towards textiles, with an unhealthy interest in batique). She got high marks, and was called to a meeting with
she hadn't paid her fees and the college wanted to help her to get onto the degree course of her choice. As we did't have a spare
oosed her as fictitious, and got into a fair amount of trouble.
, my work, while physically looking a bit random and incoherent, shares the same kind of interest in the mismatch of what ar
what it appears to be, or claims to be, in the way that Frances Neil did. So I've been making hyper-real statues of those buskers
to be statues, which actively make money on the street. I've been copying and re-configuring objects, from cutting all the leaves
re, or painting abstract-expressionist versions of magic-eye images, to re-arranging all the words in the Bible into alphabetica
en re-spraying abandoned and burned-out vehicles in the street. I've been re-recording utopian songs by people who have
eal lives, as if they were recorded before the original (like Lennon's 'Imagine' done by a '60s motown girl-group etc...). I've been
e statuettes of seminal moments in performance art, and 'life-size' physical versions of cartoon thought-bubbles. I re-chromed
scooter, and carved full-size trees out of wood, and rocks out of stone. And as language and utopias are both fine examples o
between an idea and it's reality, and never quite do what they are trying to do, i'm hoping to graffitti the entire text of Sir Thomas

(Flora) 2002 wax fibreglass clothes hair and paint

Piaggio(metalic pink) 2002 burnt out scooter and spray paint

Transit (diamond white) 2002 abandoned van and paint

Saxo(signal yellow) 2002 burnt out car and spray paint

Sierra (ocean blue) 2002 abandoned car and spray paint

The wood for the trees 2005-6 carved wood and stone

Rosie Snell
born 1971 Littlehampton
studied Loughborough College of Art & Design and Norwich School of Art & Design
lives and works London
represented by Vertigo Gallery

Ambush 2004 oil on canvas on panel 178 x 229 cm

Reconnaissance 2006 oil on canvas on panel 111 x 165 cm

Stealth Tactics 2001 oil on canvas on panel 109 x 163 cm

Stalker 2005 oil on canvas on panel 163 x 163 cm

Samuel Wale c1760 *Robert Kett under the Oak of Reformation* oil on canvas courtesy of Norwich Castle Museum and Art Gallery

Ruth Ewan

Brian Higgins
Producer and Songwriter
Xenomania

5th March 2006

Dear Mr Higgins,

I am an artist based in London. Currently I am working on a project entitled *The Rebels' Complaint* which will be shown as part of *East International* at the Norwich Gallery later this year. *The Rebels' Complaint* will take the form of a commissioned song telling the romantic and tragic story of Robert Kett, leader of the Norfolk Rising of 1549, which was sparked by the fencing off of common land by local gentry. During the summer of 1549 Kett declared parliament under a tree known as the Oak of Reformation that still stands on Mousehold Heath, approximately one mile from the city of Norwich, where he tried the landowners. By the winter of 1549 foreign mercenaries were brought in and the crown prevailed over the English peasants. Kett was executed outside Norwich Castle while nine of his men were hung, drawn and quartered under the Oak of Reformation. Kett is now widely regarded as a local hero. Having read that your pop production factory, Xenomania, stands for 'everything about the interesting side of music but with tunes the postman will whistle', I would like to invite you to work with me in order to create the song.

The aspect of music I find most interesting is its ability to be used as a learning tool, it combines three effective techniques of persuasion: a trusted voice, sublimity and repetition. No amount of historical reading could inspire such emotive feeling as songs such as the Special AKA's 'Nelson Mandela', Ewan MacColl's 'Derek Bentley' or Nina Simone's 'Strange Fruit', to name but a few. As a pop production house I believe Xenomania has the power to bring the story of Robert Kett into the wider public psyche allowing the legend of the rebellion to disseminate into popular culture. By creating this song I would like not only produce a 'tune that the postman will whistle' but one that he will be inspired to sing aloud to with conviction. As you have been hailed 'the Phil Spector of the 21st century' and have a reputation for 'packing avant-garde surprises into three chart topping minutes' I invite you to use this subject for a hit of a new dimension.

I have enclosed an early example of 'The Land Song' c.1900 which may be of interest, along with a picture of Kett under the Oak of Reformation and the tree as it stands today. I look forward to hearing what you think about the idea.

Yours sincerely

Ruth Ewan

A MARCHING SONG FOR LAND REFORMERS.

Air—"Marching through Georgia."

Tree on Mousehold Heath Norwich thought to be the Oak of Reformation

Theresa Nanigian
born 1961 Boston
studied National College of Art & Design and Dublin Institute of Technology
lives and works Dublin

46 missed manicures

Do not complain, do not rejoice, try to understand.[1]
Spinoza

At the core of Theresa Nanigian's video work is an investigation into the disjunction between the mediated versions of major world events and their impacts on 'ordinary' lives. She uses the tools and language of highly developed data recording systems to ask a different set of questions and to present a different set of facts. Working against the hyper reality of the media spectacle presented by single perspective strategies, which only serve to intensify and flatten, Nanigan's survey moves beyond its epicentre. She follows a different track, tracing the ripple effects and touching on the nuanced fragments – the splinter statistics – of a 'catastrophe's' aftermath. The resulting work – *'46 missed manicures'* – is an evenly paced - seemingly random - sequence of texts, listing factual information in small white letters against a pure black background. Each affirmation, given without context, opens up another narrative and provides another clue – like pieces of a jigsaw – the unfolding scene interweaving between the significant and seemingly insignificant, oddball facts resonating from 9/11. A slow realisation dawns, as the evidence put forth brings us in a quiet and understated way to feelings of a more intimate sadness and loss. The clinical format of statistic gathering is at once utilised and subverted by Nanigian in her aim to bring us closer to the underlying shards of reality. The spare simplicity of her texts resist any sentimentality or sensationalist seduction and leaves room to breathe, giving a space to think on - the manifold repercussions, multiple entryways, the unexpected connections within a single incident.

> "46 missed manicures
> 500 cases of red, white and blue M&M's distributed
> 16 forty-three foot palm trees destroyed
> 1,300 orphans
> 2,900 coffee chain stores receive voicemail message
>   from chief executive
> 100 unemployed actors…"

The work is the artist's personal response to the September 11th terrorist attacks on the World Trade Centre, New York. Nanigian lived in the city and worked in the Atrium at the World Financial Centre, which is next door to the Twin Towers. She has said of this work, that it is amongst her more personal and she made it because she felt the need to work out her own feelings to the overwhelming event. Her sense of 'loss' and a desire to understand, what had been made possible to *imagine* by compulsive repetition of TV images of planes slicing into the Twin Towers, of the Twin Towers imploding in what has been called by one thinker "Mother of all events"[2]. How do you cover the unthinkable? How do you find a way through the hysterical media's portrait, the collapse of the Twin Towers, the apex of Western global power and wealth, that apocalyptic scene?

Nanigian's methodologies function as inventories. A former strategic management consultant and business analyst she is a dedicated 'list-maker' and has used her capacities in this field to create a form of artistic production and critique that is relevant for the contemporary context. Whereas the business analyst sets out to 'isolate' and then solve a situation or a problem through data collection and evaluation, Nanigian operating as artist-analyst works in reverse. By asking the questions others forget to ask such as what people planned to do on 'the day' and what they actually did, her inquiry moves beyond the pursuit of mere facts or hardcore information, and she presents within her script insights into the smaller threads; slivers of a continuous and disjointed narrative. It is in her "interest for communication"[3], for remembering, for making some small sense of the loss, that this "survey" reads more like poetry. In a very modest way *'46 missed manicures'* removes layers of celluloid's artifice to locate something real, genuine, buried deep.

© Clíodhna Shaffrey February 2006

[1] For an excellent reflection on 9/11 see Richard Kearney's chapter on Terror in *Strangers Gods & Monsters*, Routledge, 2003. He asks 'How can we understand the 'terror'? He makes his attempt with Spinoza's maxim in mind: "Do not complain, do not rejoice, try to understand".

[2] Jean Baudrillard in his essay, *'The Spirit of Terrorism'*, Verso, 2002, the collapse of the Twin Towers was he claimed the 'Mother of all events' in that it symbolized the supreme *suicidal* act not just of the terrorists but of Western global capital itself.

[3] Kearney, Richard. *Strangers Gods and Monsters*, Routledge, 2003, (chapter The Immemorial: A Task of Narrative) p. 182 Kearney quotes from Habermas, who refers to narrative's (*mythos – mimesis*) capacity to call out to the other - to be on its way to the other - as *interest for communication* – an interest which goes beyond a mere interest for facts or information. 'To engage in a narrative history – as oppose to a purely statistical record – is to enlarge our sphere for communication and connection with others'.

30,000 cups of coffee not served

26 mentions at the 4 hour, 25 minute Oscar ceremony

500 refrigerated trucks dispatched

1,261 empty seats at the opera

12% report children with nightmares and 33% who are easily annoyed

20% increase in births nine months on

91% approval rating for the major

331 captives

500 cases of red, white and blue M&Ms distributed

39% would allow government agencies to monitor the telephone calls
of ordinary citizens

1,300 orphans

10 passengers removed from train and questioned for 1 hour, 40 minutes

17 babies born fatherless

two-thirds of teenagers feel closer to their families

42% of readers want suspect executed

1,616 certificates issued without a body

$20 Frequent Flyer Bra marketed in response to security alerts
caused by bra underwires

22,000 bombs

16 fourtythree-foot palm trees destroyed

100 unemployed actors

92 days before first related suicide

1,640,000 tons of debris

two weeks and sixteen sundays in between

In 'two weeks and sixteen sundays in between', Theresa Nanigian films the sky onto which she then superimposes headline clippings from two newspapers – the Irish Times and the New York Times. The project began as an experiment in which Nanigian sets out to explore feelings of displacement and distance between media coverage of news and their impact on actual feelings of 'being in the world". Using herself as 'subject' – she recorded daily a morning ritual of reading the papers and looking at the sky from her backyard. Her experiment asks that she would relinquish control over material gathered – the impossibility of knowing beforehand either news or weather (skies), made the process from the start unpredictable. However, what began as a testing ground and format for note taking soon unfolded into a definite narrative as her project coincided with the swift build up to the invasion by the US of Iraq, the war in Iraq and 'after' the war. The other newspaper headlines logged during this period deal with 'local' matters - the peace process in Northern Ireland; the health service; the standardisation of the school year; the relations between Ireland and the US. They appear out of sync and interrupt the emerging narrative, throwing us off course, dissolving any fixed content.

Nanigian's film was made over the course of two weeks and sixteen Sundays from January to March 2003. In a very short span of time we come full circle: before the war; after the war. Her experiment posits the speed of information technology with the *speed of war*[1]. The movement of news around a 'shrinking' globe makes distance and surface irrelevant, collapsing time and space, media and reality, which we have been told contribute to feelings of alienation and loss. Yet Nanigian's film, which captures this very speed at work, also retrieves a meaning out of daily headlines, and works against media's neutralising effect. Her composition of pure sky – without horizon – is tinged with an ominous undercurrent, as darkness filters through light. The headline news now emancipated from its source (newspaper) and repositioned against the heavens builds a separate narrative and opens other meanings, allows for further questions. The innocent sky – transcendent, liminal, sublime - is also flight path, war route and airspace. An unconscious decoding of sign and text occurs as fleeting background sounds - a child's voice, church bells, birdsong - hint at distance and connection. These familiar sounds - grounded in 'everyday normality' occupy a different space, another reality, and yet imbue a strange mix of melancholia and comfort. Their invisible presences appear at once part of and apart from the given scene. A bell tolls as 'taxi suicide blast kills four'. Somewhere between text and image thoughts move from the political - on war and death; on war and economy; on the US military planes, which the Irish government permits to land in Shannon;

on the fact that a 'continuing' war is declared 'over'; - to the metaphysical - on *being and nothingness*; on the possibility/impossibility of a beyond, on transience and temporality. 'two weeks and sixteen sundays in between' might be viewed as a requiem - a requiem for Iraq, a requiem for an illegal war. It might also read as a study of sky and of the possibility of mysterious interconnections and a coincidental underlying unity. And it might read as recognition of the 'self' living somewhere in translation between different planes of reality.

Nanigian's experiment carried out in her backyard underneath mutable Irish skies reveals a possibility for the co-existence of different layers of meaning hidden between text, image and being. She suggests a possibility to simultaneously experience disjointed feelings, thoughts and information and at the same time not loose touch with a day-to-day reality. It is as if both connected and disconnected to the turbulent world around that the self is liberated from any fixed position or imagined unity. The overload and speed of information technologies, which have given rise to a new order of the media – where text, code, sign predominate, signalling a 'death of the real' - are for sure powerful, omnipresent and determining. But in Nanigian's film, cut out news headlines repositioned onto a film of sky, leaves space for imagining. In 'two weeks and sixteen sundays in between' we come closer to the (sur)realism underpinning our contemporary 'fragmented' era where it is possible to float in and out of overlapping realities, where meanings are slippery, freeplay, diverse and seldom fixed. Where it is as possible to have feelings for or care about 'things' that are happening far away, and at the same time, tune out, switch off and refocus on what is near to hand. In a beautiful and spare work Theresa Nanigian throws open a complexity within and without.

© Clíodhna Shaffrey March 2006

[1] Paul Virillio is inventor of the term 'dromology', meaning the logic of speed that is the foundation of technological society. His major works include *War and Cinema*, *Speed and Politics* and *The Information Bomb* in which he argues, among many other things, that military projects and technologies drive history – 'history progresses at the speed of its weapons systems' (Speed and Politics). In Anthony Swoffords *Jarhead; A Marine's Chronicle to the Gulf War and Other Battles*, he makes explicit Virillio's assertion - of the speed of conflict and the contraction of time and space under the impact of technology – with this first hand account of the conflict 'on the ground' by one marine. "Hell I don't know if we'll be needed. The war's going to be moving too fast. Sixteen hundred yards is nothing. Sixteen hundred yards was two weeks fighting in Vietnam and a whole goddamn year in World War 1. I'll last about five minutes out here, if you ask me."

Tom Ranahan
born 1963 Birmingham
studied Stoke-on-Trent
lives and works in Birmingham

Joyland

By way of introduction, Tom Ranahan's pictures of Great Yarmouth – which, if you were brought up in Britain in the 70s, connect uneasily with memories of holidaying as a child – address the reality of what seaside towns have become. In one sense, Yarmouth has become a caricature of itself, and the place has a double-edged identity that clings to a strange semblance of reality. The town's Britishness is essential to this split personality; its comic amateurness rendering any easy journey into pure fantasy farcical, hovering as it does in an edgy no-man's land. Another view of the place might exist in a myopic reduction of the town's rawness through a nostalgia for a lost Britain, and the dream of a more honest and simple past, an idea perhaps based on a sympathy for outmoded forms of entertainment. And this is where Tom's photographs come in. Locating themselves outside both of these perspectives, the beauty in his images is in their incidental banality: there are no over-played theatrics, nothing to do with ideas around the philistine, no social anthropology or distant documentary style. These pictures simply describe extraordinary places.

Take for example *Joyland I* and *Joyland II* (both 2005), which present straightforward images of a fun fair. The photographs are taken from the road, and *Joyland II* shows a cartoon fibreglass landscape populated by spooks and ghouls, as well as clowns and soft animals. The most successful of these elements is a rocket that's somehow embedded itself in the roof of the building – or in the grass bank of the fictional landscape. This spaceship also appears in *Joyland I*, which is perhaps the more unusual of the two pictures. The amusement park's gates stand at the centre of the frame, as does a modern Toyota van – and it's this inappropriate invasion of normality, or unnatural jump, that gives the picture a strange form of pathos. What's this vehicle doing in the picture, corrupting the already implausible nature of its subject matter?

Similarly another photograph, *Stairway to Heaven* (2005), shows a brick staircase that's been dug into a grass bank leading from the beach. It stops, quite abruptly, halfway down the slope. Positioned at the top of the incline with its two columns reaching to the sky, it's at once a celestial gateway to the heavens, and an awkward unfinished mistake brought about by council cutbacks.

As a native of Birmingham, it's not surprising that Ranahan's become interested in the diverse excess of seaside culture. His own city in the Midlands is the only major landlocked metropolis in the country without a natural centre point or a river running through it. Ranahan's home is fragmented and, until recently – before massive redevelopment took place – seemed beautifully without direction. The last few years have seen a massive change in the city's landscape and fortunes. The old Bull Ring's gone, and a lot of the more unusual local character has been thrown out with it. Tom's had his studio in the city centre's adjoining area of Digbeth for the past fifteen years, and he's been documenting the renovation of factories, the wholesale demolition of buildings, as well as the stubborn refusal of certain parts of the area to give up the ghost. In this sense, both Birmingham and Yarmouth occupy a grey area of perception: at one moment depressed and highly strung, on another, elated and at one with the world.

Tom is a close friend of Ian Skoyles, an artist whose work was included in EAST in 2001. Ian was raised in Yarmouth in the 60s and 70s, but settled in Birmingham in the 80s. When Ian was in Norwich, Tom visited Yarmouth and took his initial photographs. Printed only in late 2005, their frankness proved to show an unnaturally powerful melancholy, not only through their delayed formation, but also by way of their honesty and humour.

The majority of Tom's new photographs are slightly different from these initial images, but share the same subject matter. Having been taken this year, they intend to push his concern with seaside entertainment further. One hope is that they'll take a fresh look at Yarmouth, and present a rare view of the place and its surrounding area. Another is that they might continue to evade any overbearing interpretation, and reveal more magical, disturbing and honest views of the artificial culture that lies at the heart of our seaside towns.

© Andrew Hunt 2006

Boat off Yarmouth Beach 2005 photograph 101.5 x 122 cm

Joyland II 2005 photograph 61 x 91.5 cm
Joyland I 2005 photograph 61 x 91.5 cm

Stairway to Heaven 2005 photograph 101.5 x 122 cm
Britannia Pier 2005 photograph 101.5 x 122 cm

Vaast Colson
born 1977 Kapellen Belgium
studied Royal Academy of Fine Arts Antwerp and Post St Joost Autonoom Breda
lives and works Antwerp

"Though A Lie Be Swift, The Truth Overtakes It."

Ten fibs I told as a child:

I got bitten by a snake once, luckily it wasn't poisonous

I had a jiu jiutsu black belt 2nd dan at the age of 10

my first skateboard was an authentic Zorlac

I played professional cricket and occasionally some
field hockey when residing Down Under

I spotted a small fish whilst scuba diving, the fish turned
out to be a baby shark...

I broke my leg on the goal post during soccer practice

egg in pocket story

I saw Magnum PI driving his red Ferrari in Hawaii

I pressed the alarm button in a five-star hotel elevator

I was the young champion of the Grächen Goldski Race

Hanging Shed 19 April until 19 May 2004
installation for the exhibition *A Temporary Monument for David McComb*
curated by Jean Bernard Koeman, STUK, Leuven (B)

A reconstruction of an Australian sheepshed, in which the Triffids recorded their fourth album *In the Pines*
Slides from Colsons childhood 'down-under' and mixtapes evoke loss, distance and longing

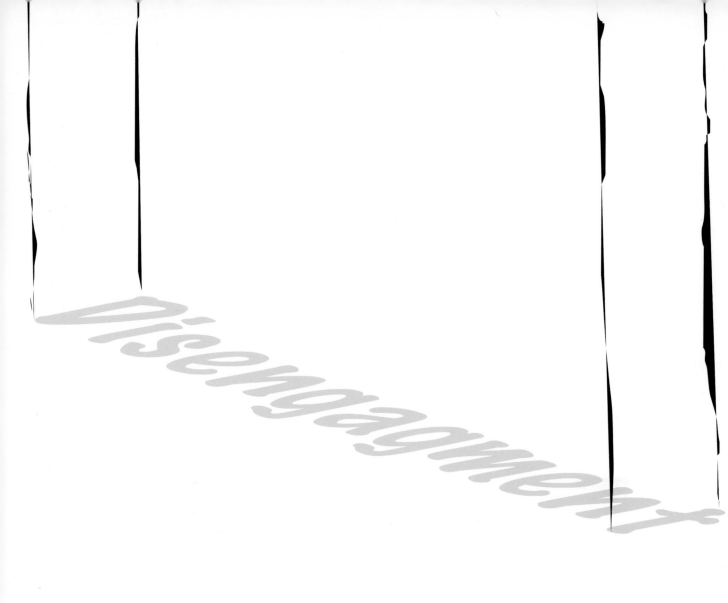

Manifesto

Yara El-Sherbini
born 1978 Derbyshire
studied UWE and the Slade
lives and works London
www.yaraelsherbini.com

Suspended disengagment

consi stant

CONARTTEXT

ward ward ward ward ward
ward ward ward ward ward
ward ward ward

ward ward

1991 **EAST**	selectors Alexander Moffat and Andrew Brighton	
1991 **EAST**award	Sandy Guy	
1992 **EAST**	selectors Helen Chadwick and Marjorie Allthorpe-Guyton	
1992 **EAST**award	Victoria Arney and Naomi Dines	
1993 **EAST**	selectors David Tremlett and Konrad Fischer	
1993 **EAST**award	Kenny Hunter	
1994 **EAST**	selectors Jan Dibbets and Rudi Fuchs	
1994 **EAST**award	Stephanie Smith	
1995 **EAST**	selectors Giuseppe Penone and Marian Goodman	
1995 **EAST**award	Mary Evans	
1996 **EAST**	selectors Richard Long and Roger Ackling	
1996 **EAST**award	Jacqueline Mesmaeker	
1997 **EAST**	selectors Nicholas Logsdail and Tacita Dean	
1997 **EAST**award	Tomoko Takahashi	
1998 **EAST**	selectors Alan Charlton and Michel Durand-Dessert	
1998 **EAST**award	Martin McGinn	
1999 **EAST**	selectors Peter Doig and Roy Arden	
1999 **EAST**award	Lucy McKenzie	
1999 **riverside**	Cornford & Cross, Elizabeth Wright, Kjetil Berge, Tazro Niscino and Tom Woolford	
2000 **EAST**	selectors Keith Piper and Sebastian Lopez	
2000 **EAST**award	Hew Locke and Jananne Al-Ani	
2000 **riverside**	Anne Rook, Christina McBride, Claudia Schmacke, James Chinneck and Nina Pope & Karen Guthrie	
2001 **EAST**	selectors Mary Kelly and Peter Wollen	
2001 **EAST**award	Zarina Bhimji	
2002 **EAST**	selectors Lawrence Weiner and Jack Wendler	
2002 **EAST**award	Adam Blumberg, Clare Iles, Hiraki Sawa, Jessica Jackson Hutchins and Milohnic & Paschke	
2003 **EAST**	selectors Toby Webster and Eva Rothschild	
2003 **EAST**award	Richard Hughes	
2003 **EAST**work	commission Matthew Houlding	
2003 **EAST**work	multiples commission Slimvolume Poster Publication	
2004 **EAST**	selectors Neo Rauch and Gerd Harry Lybke	
2004 **EAST**award	Justin Mortimer	
2004 **EAST**work	commission Christopher Landoni	
2004 **EAST**work	multiples commission Hurvin Anderson, Anja Schrey, Christiane Baumgartner, Christophe Ruckhäberle and Rose Wylie	
2005 **EAST**	selector Gustav Metzger	
2005 **EAST**award	divided between all artists	

**2005 selector
Gustav Metzger**

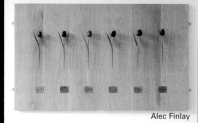
Alec Finlay

Asnat Austerlitz

Bernard Debaillie

Bryan Parsons Corinna Till Eddie Farrell
Gil Pasternak Graham Hayward

Carrie Levy

Dan Tombs

Daniel Bell

David Burrows & Simon O'Sullivan

John Kelly

Doug Fishbone

Jill Miller

Kaori Nakayama

Lee Holden

Making Things Better

Mark Wilsher

Melissa Bliss

Michael Takeo Magruder

Mustafa Hulusi & JJ Charlesworth

Peter Kennard & Cat Picton Phillipps

Sarah Pickering

Simon Faithfull

Simon Morris

Riichi Yamaguchi

tenantspin & Alan Dunn

The People Speak

**2004 selectors
Neo Rauch
Gerd Harry Lybke**

Wolfgang Fiel

Alicia Paz

Anja Schrey EASTwork

Anja Schrey

Christiane Baumgartner

Christiane Baumgartner EAST*work*

Christopher Landoni EAST*work*

TRINK HALLE

Christoph Ruckhäberle

Christoph Ruckhäberle EAST*work*

Daniela Brahm

Eric Fong

Etienne Zack

Frank Ahlgrimm

Hurvin Anderson EAST*work*

Hurvin Anderson

Jakub Dolejš

Janice McNab

John Timberlake

Justin Mortimer EAST*award*

Jennifer Walters

Jo Mitchell

Martin Kobe

Karen Brett

Lela Budde

Liz Nicol

Mikael Eriksson

Ridley Howard

Rose Wylie

Rose Wylie EAST*work*

Sean Dawson

Rosa Loy

Simon Collins

Susanne Kühn

Trish Morrissey

Sven Braun

Toril Brancher

2003 selectors
Toby Webster
Eva Rothschild

Alex Frost

Alex Graham

Alex Pollard

Camilla Løw

Caroline De Lannoy

Christopher Landoni

Christopher Wraith

Colin Lowe and Roddy Thomson

Elise Ferguson

Craig Kucia

Francis Lamb

Gareth Jones

Gregor Wright

James Pyman

Karla Black

Kate Davis

Lawrence Corby

Lorna Macintyre

Lynn Hynd

Matthew Houlding EAST*work*

Michael Stumpf

Mark Pearson

Markus Amm

Martin Poyner

Richard Hughes EAST*award*

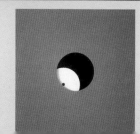
Nike Savvas

Peter McDonald

Ruth Claxton

Sara MacKillop

Simon Bloor   Slimvolume EAST*work*

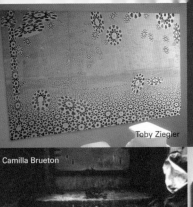
Toby Ziegler

2002 selectors
Lawrence Weiner
Jack Wendler

Adam Blumberg EAST Award

Anna Jóhannsdóttir & Ólöf Oddgeirsdót

Camilla Brueton

Christian Siekmeier

Christine Erhard

Clare Iles EAST Award

Daniel Mrohnic/Dirk Paschke EAST Award

Hiraki Sawa EAST Award

Gaia Persico

Graham Seaton

Heike Klussmann

Jessica Jackson Hutchins EAST Award

Helena Ben-Zenou

João Louro

Matthew Houlding

Raúl La Cava

PRODUCED BY STANLEY KUBRICK

Manuel Saiz

Mary Longford

Stephen Monger

Stuart Taylor

2001 selectors
Mary Kelly
Peter Wollen

Abigail Hunt

Adam Kossoff

and people always think there's hope.

Andrew Grassie

Anne-Marie Creamer

Blaise Drummond

Esteban Pastorino

Florian Zeyfang

Ian Skoyles

Johannes Maier

k r buxey

Karen Knorr

Kenny Berger

Klaus Weh

Laura Gannon

Lun*na Menoh

Mairead O'Heocha

Margaret Morgan

Mikey Cuddihy

MILITANTER WIDERSTAND *heute?*

Militant Resistance – today

Oliver Ressler

Robert Henderson

Simon Morle

2000 selectors
Keith Piper
Sebastion Lopez

Suky Best

Zarina Bhimji EAST Award

Ajam

Alessandra Andrini

Arnaud Desjardin

Art in Ruins

Midland Bank

Carl Jaycock

Christopher Stewart

Erika Tan

Eugene Palmer

Frances Goodman

Harold Offeh

Hew Locke EAST Award

Jananne Al-Ani EAST Award

Keith Thompson

Lorrice Douglas

finger artist

Lyn Lowenstein

Meera Chauda

Meschac Gaba

Ming Wong

Neil Conroy & Lesley Sanderson

Peter Zangrillo

...hel Garfield

Shona Illingworth

Simon Tegala

Tamara Stuby

Tamara Stu...

Annual Report
One Year of My Life in Statistic...

...ronique Chance

Christina McBride

Wendelien van Oldenborgh

riverside 2000
Keith Piper
Sebastian Lopez
riverside 1999
Peter Doig
Roy Arden

Anne Rooké

Claudia Schmacke

James Chinneck

Nina Pope & Karen Guthrie

Cornford & Cross

Elizabeth Wright

Kjetil Berge

Tazro Nisdino

Tom Woolford

1999 selectors
Peter Doig
Roy Arden

Alan Brooks

Anna Hunt

WOULD YOU BE WORRIED
IF ONE OF THESE
NORTHERNERS CEASED
TO EXIST?
BANK POSTER

BANK

Common Culture

David Rayson

George Shaw

Hendrik Wittkopf

Howard Ursuliak

Jaime Gili

Kaye Donachie

Janice Kerbel

Jules Mylius

Lucy McKenzie EAST Award

Marc Aldinger

Martin Westwood

Merlin James

Neil Taylor

Oliver Zwink

Paul Housley

Roger Kelly

Ron Terada

Runa Islam

Sadie Murdoch

Sarah Staton

Steven Shearer

1998 selectors
Alan Charlton
Michel Durand-Desert

Tim Stoner

Tommy Stockel

Albert Weis

Angie Anakis

Brian Cyril Griffiths

Chris Gibbons

Colin Hitchmough

Duncan Ganley

Harriet Wölki

Heather Steele

Hiroko Ichihara

Katrin Böhm

Lyndal Jefferies

Ian Whittlesea

Lucy Wood

Marit Følstad

Martin Fletcher

Martin McGinn EAST Award

Michael Simpson

Monika Oeschler

Ralf Werner

Ranko Bonn

Saki Satom

Stefano Pisano

Stephen Bram

Tomoya Yamaguchi

Tazro Niscino

1997 selectors
Nicholas Logsdail
Tacita Dean

Alex Landrum

Alexander & Susan Maris

Andrea Knobloch

Anneke De Boer

Anthony Freestone

Christoph Hafner & Miquel Valdasquin

Cornford and Cross

David Batchelor

Gavin Wade

Jamie Wagg

Joanne Moar

Judith Dean

Laura Emsley

Liesbeth Bik & Jos van der Pol

Louise Short

Margaret Barron

Mike Kay

Masakatsu Kondo

Mark Hosking

Norika Honda

Obuabang

Olga Adelantado Alvarez

Peter Fillingham

Phyllida Barlow

Phillipine Hoegen

Richard Torchia

Sa'ad Hirri

Simon Granger

Stephen Hughes

Willie McKeown

Tomoko Takahashi EAST Award

1996 selectors
Richard Long
Roger Ackling

Annette Robinson

Beth Derbyshire

Caroline Boggis

Catherine Delaney

Christine Hatt

Colin Hitchmough

David Cushway

ROIDERY THREAD STITCHED TO BUS SEATS IN
VICH, MATCHING BOTH IN COLOUR AND
NSION THE EXISTING PATTERN OF THE FABRIC.

Dean Hughes

Dré Wapenaar

Edward Chell

Erik Odijk

Hilary Brown

Jacqueline Mesmaeker EAST Award

Janet Hodgson

Judith Frost

Karsten Bott

Keith Wilson

Leo de Goede

Lothar Götz

Madeleine Strindberg

Martin Creed

Mary McIntyre

Neil Chapman

Peter Mutschler

Piotr Zamojski

Plamen Dejanov & Svetlana Heger

Rosie Leventon

Shelly Kelly

Stuart Cumberland

Tom Benson

Trevor Sutton

Valentin Hauri

Veronica Ryan

1995 selectors
Marian Goodman
Giuseppe Penone

Alain Sonneville

projecting a videotape

on top of the glass of

the frame of a ...

lexander Stengel
unich / Germany   slide N°

Carol Robertson

Claudia Terstappen

Christine Kummer

Writers' Residence and High Power, Short-wave Broadcast
Facility for a Promontory Overlooking the City

The depicted facility, comprising a guest residence and
500 kilowatt transmitter with its associated antenna
array, is to be permanently dedicated to the purpose of
broadcasting various forms of literature. Resident guest
writers would be free to use the facility at their own
discretion and, if so desiring, to broadcast their choice
of materials or readings.

To protect its occupants from the possibly harmful
effects of electro-magnetic fields the residence is to be
encased in a 'Faraday Cage' consisting of an anodised
aluminum sheathing grounded to earth.

Daniel Congdon

Colette Urban

Daniel Laskarin

David Ostrem

David Reid

Eponce

Gert Verhoeven

Gary Woodley

Gianni Plescia

Jeremy Deller

Joseph Zehrer

Klaus Gärtner

Leo Fitzmaurice

Manuel Saiz

Marcus Richards

Martina Klein

Mary Evans EAST Award

Massimo Bartolini

Mathius Fuchs & Sylvia Eckermann

Philip Stephens

Rasheed Araeen

Sarah Chilvers

Su Grierson

Simon Poulter

Stephen Waddell

Teresa Hubbard & Alexander Birchler

Tony Rickaby

Victoria Hall

Zoi Kakouri

1994 selectors
Jan Dibbets
Rudi Fuchs

Adam Colton

Alexander Guy

Allan Boston

Andrew Stahl

Andy Frost

Beat Klein

David Powell

Gabriel Weissmann

George Blacklock

Hugh Hamshaw-Thomas

Jocelyn Clarke

Kathleen Thompson

Kris Scholz

Lara Schnitger

Maggie Jennings

Mark Francis

Mark Joyce

Mark Monaghan

Matthew Higgs

Michael Grant

Michael Kirkman

Paul Butler

Paul Harrison & John Wood

Paul Kuzemczak

Pavel Büchler

Pete Smithson

Peter John

Reggy Gunn

Roger Clarke

Rose Wylie

Roy Oxlade +1991

Sandra Hastenteufel

Stephanie Smith EAST Award

Tatyana Jassovich

1993 selectors
Konrad Fischer
David Tremlett

Timothy Hyman +1991

Alison Turnbull

Bé van der Heide

Ben Cook

Benjamin Cockett

Charlie Holmes

Christine Hatt

Claudia Terstappen

David Goard

David Green

David Oates

Doreen Wilder

Gabriel Weissmann

Graham Chorlton

Greg Lucas & Dizzy Howard

James Gibson

Jane Wheeler

James Reilly

Jeff Luke

Jez Noond

Jim Hamlyn

Lucy Heyward

Kenny Hunter EAST Award

Michael Stubbs

Pádraig Timoney

Pete Smith

Peter Oxenburgh Noble

Richard Bowskill

Richard Green

Sean Taylor

Silke Hennig

Timothy Davies

Trevor Sutton

Tunde Hall

1992 selectors
Helen Chadwick
Marjorie
Allthorpe-Guyton

Alison Gill

Amy Eshoo

Andrew Herman

Anne-Marie Creamer + 1995 2001

MOSCOW

PUSHKINO

Brian Deighton

Bruce Williams

Caroline Broadhead

Claudia Berna

Davide Cantoni

Derek Tyman

Dimitri Vangrunderbeek

Edwina Fitzpatrick

Emma Rushton

Eugene Palmer

Geoff Yeomans +1994

Georgia Hayes

Hannah Horsfall & Malcolm Bell

Heather Allen

Hilary Brown

James Evans

Jane Harris

Jiro Osuga

John McCaffrey Angela McCaffrey

Jordan Baseman

Karen Williams

Katharine Dowson

PETER WONT GO TO THE BARBER

Len Shelley

Marc Atkins

Mark Joyce

Matthew Stradling

Max Fenton

Miranda Housden +1991

Naomi Dines EAST Award

Nigel Freake

Nigel Prince

Paul Rodgers

Rachel Atherton

Rebecca Fortnum

Robert Mason

Rosie Leventon

Samira Abbassy

Shirley Chubb

Stephen Hepworth

Suzanne Willey

Tim Courage

Victoria Arney EAST Award

1991 selectors
Andrew Brighton
Sandy Moffat

Alex Boardman

Alexander Guy EAST Award

Amanda Benson

Andy Barker

Andrew Sloan

Angela McCaffrey

Anne Finlayson

Antonio Bellotti

Brigitte Jurack

Christine Gist

Caroline Jupp

Christopher Cook

David Batchelor

David Hosie

David Lintine

Fred Crayk

Gordon Senior

Graham Fagen

CHASM

VOID

Graham Stewart

Helen Ballardie

Jane Dixon

Former & Form

Jim Mooney

John Capstack

John Foster

John McCaffrey

Jon Butterworth

Jordan Baseman

Kathleen Hyndman

Kevin Mount

Kevin Slingsby

Laetitia Yhap

Margaret Hunter

Mark Eyre

Nicholas Ward

Milena Tadini

Neil Hanger

Neil Patterson

Nicola Burrell

Paul Eachus

Peter Berwick

Peter Blunsden

Peter John

Peter Sansom

Peter Wilson

Philip Palmer

Philip Tyler

Rachel Budd

Roderic Barrett

Rodger Brown

Roy Trollope

Siobhan Davies

Stella Jane Tripp

Stephen Boyd

Steve Farrell

Susan Ball

Susan Campbell

Tai-Shan Schierenberg